D0573524

Reflections of Mind

Reflections

of Mind

Western Psychology Meets
Tibetan Buddhism

Tarthang Tulku
Editor

Dharma Publishing

NYINGMA PSYCHOLOGY SERIES

1. *Reflections of Mind*
2. *Gesture of Balance*
3. *Openness Mind*
4. *Kum Nye Relaxation, Parts 1 and 2*
5. *Skillful Means*
6. *Hidden Mind of Freedom*
7. *Knowledge of Freedom*

Series Editor: Tarthang Tulku
Manuscript Editor: Elsa First
Contributing Editor: Steve Tainer
Illustrator: Arthur Okamura
Photography: Eric Meller
and Dharma Publishing staff

Second edition 1989
ISBN: 0–913546–15–1; 0–913546–14–3 (pbk)
Library of Congress Catalog Card number: 75–5254

Typeset in Fototronic Times Roman and printed
in the United States of America by Dharma Press

10 9 8 7 6

This book is dedicated to the Human Development Training Program, the Nyingma Institute, and Dharma Publishing, that they may provide avenues of insight into the nature of the mind.

Contents

Foreword

The teachings of Tibetan Buddhism are the result of over 2000 years of investigating the mind. Its psychology depends on our directly inspecting the nature of inner experience and taking responsibility for the quality of our awareness.

These teachings were introduced to a group of psychologists and mental health professionals during intensive eight-week seminars which were offered at the Nyingma Institute in the summers of 1973 and 1974. The opening of the Nyingma Institute in 1973 was intended to provide a new channel for integrating the teachings of the East with Western approaches —to bring these traditional understandings of awareness within reach of modern psychological investigation and to communicate these methods as a basis for a more meaningful approach to life.

The Nyingmapa have always attempted to balance the practice of meditation with precise intellectual understanding. During the summer sessions, we discussed the fundamental theories of Nyingma philosophy and psychology and practiced a variety of physical and mental exercises to enable close observation of the mind and its various levels of consciousness.

Awareness is a vast subject, for there are many kinds of awareness which directly affect our health, our understanding, and our ability to appreciate the opportunities and possibilities of our lives. From day to day, each situation provides the means for growth in self-knowledge. At times, it is helpful to sit still—to observe and identify the many kinds of events between one thought and another, to note how the unhealthy patterns of our lives unfold, and to realize that so-called external events are intricately activated and mirrored by various manifestations of mind. Through deep meditation and intelligent exploration of the mind, awareness develops spontaneously within each situation.

Traditionally, the successful application of these teachings presumes an extensive mental training, but even in two months many people's lives were deeply affected. The summer programs have thus provided a useful beginning. The articles published in this book present the reflections of a variety of professionals who are directly concerned with helping themselves and others, and who are exploring the possibilities of integrating Tibetan Buddhist practices with their own approaches to mental health and therapy. In the future we hope to explore more advanced subjects and to consider meditative practices in greater detail.

TARTHANG TULKU

Head Lama of the Tibetan
Nyingma Meditation Center
and the Nyingma Institute

Reflections of Mind

Reflections
of Mind

Tarthang Tulku

All human situations arise through the medium of awareness. People do many things and feel many different ways,
but the central factor of all activities is always awareness.
Perhaps we do not notice the presence of this knowing
quality, or we may take it for granted. This can lead to problems. It is important for us to know that there are many kinds
of awareness, which arise according to definite principles, and
which affect our health, our understanding, and our happiness. We must take responsibility for the condition of our
awareness, since so-called external affairs correspond to this
condition very precisely. This is the basic theme running
through much of Buddhist teaching. To the extent that this

TARTHANG TULKU, RINPOCHE is a reincarnate lama and former
head of Tarthang Monastery in Eastern Tibet. He served as Professor of Buddhist Philosophy at Sanskrit University in Benares, India,
and is Founder and Head Lama of the Tibetan Nyingma Meditation Center and the Nyingma Institute in Berkeley, California.

teaching can offer understanding of the value of each type of
awareness available to us, and of the methods or circumstances which activate each type, it can be very valuable.
Pursuing this understanding is more serious and immediately
useful than casual research into 'altered states of consciousness'. Śākyamuni, the Buddha of this age, said that truly
valuable penetrating awareness is usually covered over and
forgotten by most human beings, and that this situation is like
being trapped in a burning house, oblivious to any danger.

The fall into 'unknowing'

The fall from living according to sharp, value-oriented
awareness to depending on tight, limited ways of knowing
(*ma-rig-pa*) is not an isolated event. It has many immediate
consequences. Traditionally, these consequences are represented by the eleven successive links in the Wheel of Life
which follow the fall into 'unknowing'. A terrible speed, lack
of alternatives, and loss of personal balance are essential to
this Twelve-link process ... we move helplessly from one
preoccupation to the next, never able to achieve fulfillment.
Awareness becomes a matter of being 'aware of' some situation, and none of these situations involve full satisfaction or
real clarity. We can see this driving speed in our own affairs. It
has been greatly increased by some aspects of the twentieth
century 'way of life'. In an approach to life influenced by
ma-rig-pa, human beings only accept what is presented to
them by their sensations, and this tendency is particularly
encouraged by present-day inclinations. Strangely enough,
such an attitude is accompanied by the inability to really
experience and appreciate sensations! This inability is generally due to *ma-rig-pa*, but has become very severe for people in
the West during this last century. Buddhism finds it important
to look beyond the world comprised of sensations, and does
this partly by attending to these very sensations in a thorough,
appreciative manner. We see here a very important difference
in approaches to life.

Modern education deals in ideas to the exclusion of many sensations which are essential 'food' for human development. Ideas which are given great emphasis often lack the corresponding concrete impressions and experience that the body needs to reach agreement with the intellect. Even in daily interactions and difficulties, we are concerned only with the idea of what we are doing, the idea of our difficulty. The actuality of our problem may be much easier to deal with than our concept of it . . . we will never find out until we can touch the felt qualities of our situation directly. Maybe there is no problem at all aside from our thinking about the problem. On the conceptual level, problems are self-perpetuating.

It might be useful to see what else—if anything—is going on. The pain that we feel may result from the discomfort of the body, which suffers because it is not acting in harmony with the mind. Without a proper balance of functioning between our awareness and our body, it is natural to see and feel 'problems'. In America, sports and entertainment are supposed to provide the physical relaxation and sensations that are missing elsewhere. But, in fact, these activities also promise us more than they really give—we are often left still feeling hungry for satisfying experience, tired out but not relaxed. The mind is always busy seeking some nice gift, an ideal, a 'cosmic good' which it promises to secure for the body. All it actually brings back, however, is the pain and frustration it has collected . . . this is the 'gift' which the body must accept.

As the body becomes more uncomfortable, the mind is more unwilling to come back to it and spends more time chasing its dreams. This leads to greater isolation, pain that seems to have no remedy. If our goals are based on concepts that have no experiential foundation, we will be straining our senses to seek levels of reality which forever elude us. This can result in constant frustration and very strange double standards—we might pay homage to ideals just because they are 'not like us', completely out of reach, while feeling guilty and ashamed about our own condition. And if the conduct of our lives proceeds at such a pace that there is no time to enjoy

sensations, we 'starve'. The long-term effects of such frustration and starvation can be so disorienting that a person's entire
life might amount to one great confusion, one delusion. Beginning with the pursuit of ideas, we become caught in a realm
of fascination that involves increasingly greater speed, which
produces agitation, disillusionment, and pain. Pain encourages
a separation of body and mind which leaves no possibility of
calmness, relaxation, or insight. Our awareness becomes very
dense, dark and 'stuck' . . . there is no solution in sight.

Śākyamuni described the endless turnings of the Twelve-
link Wheel as amounting to one long fitful night's dream.
We must try to wake up! Buddhism has many advanced,
sophisticated teachings, but until we have corrected this
basic lack of balance between body and mind, we cannot even
begin to 'wake up'. Our immediate sensations are the doors
to higher realizations. Good health is the first step towards
enlightenment.

In straying into a realm of confusion, we have traded an
appreciative awareness for a preoccupation with limited purposes. A vast, integrated space has become narrowed down to
a container of isolated things, including the divided mind-
body. It is necessary to reverse this tendency, but without
ignoring or perpetuating the separate elements which make
up our present world-view. As soon as we begin to be 'aware
of things', to 'see things', we have trouble. This is true in
several senses. Outwardly, being aware of some specific situation sets up a series of related identifications and desires
which eventually leads to a frustrating position. Inwardly,
when we are meditating, we may think we're having great
success because we are noting everything, counting all our
thoughts. But this is not really 'paying attention' in any high
sense . . . we are just playing games. Even when we become
more concentrated, so that we are completely immersed in our
attention, like a cat watching something, our awareness is
still stuck someplace. It is not exactly 'aware of', but it is still
narrow and kind of hypnotized. We could stay here for a long

time without falling into a frustrating place, but we are not
making any progress. So we must go beyond all awareness
which is stuck on some thing or in some place.
Yet, it would be absurd to try to avoid everything, to blot
everything out. So . . . somehow, the very things which are
disconnected, fragmented, must themselves yield up a vision
of continuity, of unity.
Trying to make this happen can also become a preoccupation . . . we need to work very lightly and subtly, not pushing too hard to do anything. If we are desperate to change our
situation, to go elsewhere, we will probably not achieve real
balance or insight. It is very similar to the more sophisticated
Western therapeutic methods. The most effective therapy
does not involve a heavy concern for 'therapizing' someone
. . . there is no fixed picture of things being 'terribly wrong'.
Making dichotomies the working basis for the discovery of
unity is really a very practical procedure, and it is the only way
our ordinary problems can be properly resolved. The human
body, which is often a solid, cramped expression of isolation
and pain, can be used to realize a more expansive awareness
and satisfaction. Our ordinary awareness, which so often mis-
treats the body, can also nourish it and encourage concrete
implementation of very profound values. It is well-known that
body and mind are a theoretical unity of some kind, but in
actual practice they may be at odds with one another.
Buddhism has many methods for beginning to work with
the fact of this antagonism. We may expose a clear, unques-
tionable unity which has great existential importance, rather
than mere formal interest. 'Mind' and 'body' may come to
have new significance for us, and may become balanced and
relaxed. Relaxation expands into calmness, the ability to
really enjoy sensations and proper functioning of the body.
This can be a very healing process. We retain tensions at
the cost of having our lives greatly shortened . . . it is better to
give our bodies the chance for long, meaningful efforts. There
is much talk now about enlightenment, but enlightenment is
not an object of distant, unearthly travels. It is a matter of

internal development that begins with good health. When we seek the 'shore beyond', this 'beyond' is only a matter of getting past the confusion of *ma-rig-pa*, not of going somewhere else.

People who are very busy and work hard to save money may think that they will take care of their body-mind at some later time, or will seek enlightenment when they have retired. But complete health and awakening are really the same, and only have meaning in terms of present action, present difficulties. Once the mind and body function separately even for a little while, discriminations arise which destroy our ability to perceive the unity of our situations. Streams of moments arise which involve patterns of discovering more and more problems, and these patterns are very hard to cut through. At this point, we *are* these patterns; we *are* the problems, so we cannot escape. If we live this way for many years, how can we then hope to discover serenity or enlightenment? It would be very terrible to become old, especially for someone who has worked for a life-time to gain material security, and be unable to practice self-care and self-healing, or to achieve self-understanding. (Buddhism teaches that from the higher point of view there is no 'self'. But as long as there is suffering, we may use the word 'self' to speak about our problems and needs. Actually, 'self-understanding' is not some concrete knowledge about something inside us, but is an on-going process of enlightening our relationship with our world. This process has no stopping-point.)

If we have no control over our health, our peace of mind, or our understanding, but must depend on others for these things, can we really feel satisfied or secure? Since so many possibilities are locked within our 'body' and 'mind', it is worthwhile for us to begin now to fully comprehend them.

The body

People awaken to one situation after another, always trying to 'be themselves'. We all respond in ways that express what we have brought to a situation, what we find there, and what we expect will follow from our actions. It is the human body that serves to 'sum up' a person's past and which asserts his attitudes toward his present and future. There are many ways in which the body keeps the traces of experience and influences all awareness according to the preserved traces.

Many different interpretations of this statement are possible by both Western sciences and the Buddhist traditions. We are talking about the more therapeutic interpretations, which say that experience may be improperly digested and may be preserved by traces which influence us even when this influence is no longer right for us. If this occurs, then the body must be purged or corrected in some way. Buddhist interpretations of 'reincarnation' and of successive existences maturing from seeds planted by our past actions also depend on a concern for cleansing our bodies of harmful 'sets'. In fact, many religions show this concern by the emphasis they place on fasting and seclusion. But in Buddhism, the methods for working with one's body and the understanding of what a 'body' really is, are different from those of other traditions.

Each human body has duration. Massage, exercise, and relaxation are considered to be good for us, in that they help us to feel and to work better in the future. For a given person, we speak of 'his' body and 'his' life-time . . . supposedly, the same person and body persist over time, and proper care of the body helps guarantee happiness for 'its owner'. This is the way we often think when we exercise. However, Buddhism —especially the Vajrayāna—maintains that the body is a matter of 'on-going embodiment'. Who we are and what we are like are embodied in each moment. There is a certain kind of awareness there, and this awareness actualizes a situation that is concretely expressed by a solid 'body' in a solid 'world'. The 'person' and the 'body' are matters of the moment. Usually embodiment follows a certain pattern through time, but this pattern could be changed. It is not true that the body is a fixed, solid thing whose duration can only involve 'more of the same'—same body, same being. The process of on-going embodiment makes it possible that our present efforts and intentions might give birth to a new 'being' in the future. According to Buddhism, we are moving from incarnation to incarnation in each succeeding instant. We can use our embodiment in this moment to produce the embodiment of Buddha-awareness.

This is not producing an 'enlightened self'. Speaking in one way though, we may develop many different kinds of higher 'bodies', including the three Kāyas of the Buddha. But this is possible only if we use our embodied existence to express every aspect of what we wish to bring into being. And before we can do that, we must be aware of the limiting factors of our present life-patterns . . . all these must be experienced and de-activated, otherwise our efforts to achieve freedom from our usual frustrations will fail. When we work to realize all that is involved in our present existence and use this knowledge to implement new values, we are practicing meditation, philosophical study, relaxation, and exercise in the Buddhist way. As examples of Buddhist practices which point out and ease our physical and mental blocks and which help us create new kinds of awareness, we may speak of Kum Nye (*sku-mnye*) and Shin Jhong (*shin-sbyong*).

Kum Nye

Kum Nye is only a beginning way of realizing a new kind of being. It is not an advanced or esoteric practice. But it is an excellent preliminary for more sophisticated Buddhist meditations, and places great emphasis on the traditional Buddhist concern with the meaning and value of the human body. It should not be done with the common attitude about 'exercise', massage, or 'yoga'. If practiced with the proper understanding, it can put us in touch with the pure energies of our situations . . . we may see that these situations are not so different from so-called 'higher realities'.

Kum Nye means 'body massage', 'body feeling'. The Tibetan word for 'body' used here does not refer to a physical machine, but to an embodiment of values, responsiveness. The teachings of the Kum Nye system are not found in the Abhidharma treatises nor among the exercises popularly called 'yoga'. Such 'yoga' may not produce real insight or relaxation, and can be like an empty gesture. Even the Abhidharma approaches may be very tense and repressed.

The Nyingma lineage has better ways, including Kum Nye exercises. In Tibet, advanced practitioners would perform Kum Nye as a 'warm up' to higher meditations. Unlike other therapeutic methods, Kum Nye uses all of man's faculties simultaneously in a skillful, harmonious way. Body, mind, breath, sound, sight, sensations, emotions—everything becomes one practice.

There are many Kum Nye exercises, but at the Nyingma Institute we teach a sequence designed especially for the problems and needs of American people. More than sixty exercises have been selected for use. Such exercises can be a very effective method of self-massage and self-healing. Some of this knowledge of pressure points and physical techniques comes from my own Gurus, and can be practiced without fear of danger or harm.

Kum Nye can be especially helpful to people who have many emotional blocks, who feel isolated, lonely, or lost. But we all need some healing method, some way of healing our life-tendencies. Even when we are first born, we have tensions and discomforts, many fears and confusions. As we become older, we seek to solve these problems by learning more and acting according to the beliefs of our society. Mostly, this means learning many ideas and developing more habits. But this develops a more solid, tight ego that wants many things and is afraid of other things. We may just have understood how to function well as adults when suddenly we find ourselves becoming old. Somehow, we never thought about this, never really prepared ourselves properly. We may become more afraid and confused, and this confusion is carried even beyond death into totally different realms. It is very important that we learn to 'heal' these patterns of living. So often we are off-balance and have nothing solid to rely on. Feeling this way, we accumulate more and more tensions which are never discharged but instead become a part of us, of our approaches to living. Kum Nye helps to expose and blow up these tensions, and to show us the more 'alive' aspects of our world. Through regular practice, a more healthy awareness can be achieved. Beginning with physical movements, which become regulated by control of breath and attention to the immediacy of our sensations, we can learn to relax.

Relaxation has many meanings in Buddhism. The Abhidharmikas, Yogācāras, and Mādhyamikas all gave this term an important place in their theories, although they understood it in quite different ways. Even for the highest stage of the Vajrayāna, the Ati-yoga, complete freedom from restless movements of awareness, complete relaxation, is the goal. For the Ati-yoga, relaxation has a connection with the idea of perfection. Perfection is usually thought of as excluding all sorts of things as being 'imperfect', but Ati-yoga uses it in the sense of embracing everything as being very fine, very positive. This understanding is far from the ego's ideas of relaxation and perfection. Ego cannot be truly relaxed, and Kum Nye should not be turned to the ego's tiring purposes. We do not have to fight the ego or make it our enemy, but it is important to take its special characteristics into account.

According to Nyingma teachings there are nine basic types of people. Each of these involves different weaknesses and ways of using meditation incorrectly. So it is important to learn Kum Nye from a teacher who can adapt these practices to one's individual needs. Some people should not perform Kum Nye. Generally, however, it is beneficial for most Americans interested in personal development. Without such a method of orientation, some central issues of meditation might not be found, or their discovery might be left to chance.

Left on our own, meditation can easily become an extension of our usual frustrating habit-patterns. This frustration cannot be removed by ignoring our emotional blockages ... only after these knots have been untied can we cultivate a more penetrating awareness.

Beginning with a preliminary stage of relaxation, we can work to attain an experience of bliss, 'emptiness', and clarity throughout the three times and the ten directions. Even unpleasant, agonizing feelings can then be accepted and included in our practice, without any attempt to ignore or therapize them away. Tibetan lineages all emphasize that 'agony' can be used to assist meditation practice. When we understand this, everything becomes 'relaxation'.

Of the nine types of people, some have greater frustration or more thoughts when they begin to practice meditation. Others have very few thoughts. Some people experience nothing unusual at all in their practice. But no matter which way we work, we have a certain difficulty. For those who become very nervous, the strong energy of the ego is covering up any clear insight into the ego's real nature. Any attempt to relax, to understand our inner nature is going against much inertia and is very threatening to something in us. Sitting practice lets loose energy which is then not being used for anything ... we don't know where to put it. We may find ourselves in a boiling cauldron of free energy, perhaps near to madness. And for those who easily find a quiet meditative state, there is a similar problem of being unable to get enough energy to see their true character clearly. One way or another, we are put off from the cultivation of penetrating insight.

This is the defense of the self-image—if there is an 'I' who is overwhelmed by blocked-up energy, who is calm, or who sees everything to be 'as usual', there seems to be no doubt as to the reality of this 'I'. We should not be so easily convinced. If we are caught up in conflicts or put to sleep by pleasant feelings, Kum Nye can wake us up in a strong but subtle way.

Tarthang Tulku, Rinpoche, founder of the Nyingma Institute and creator of the Human Development Training Program. The teachings and techniques he introduced during five intensive summer sessions became the foundation of the Kum Nye and Nyingma Training Programs now led by the Institute faculty.

Then we can carefully examine the nature of 'the meditator', 'the experiencer'. For Buddhism, these are not real entities but powerfully embodied fictions. Kum Nye is designed to break our attachment to them. It does this by increasing our awareness of the immediate feeling-tone of each item of experience, whether this is an emotion, a memory, a perceived object, a project, or a 'self'. Such attention to the givenness of the self-image greatly decreases its power. This self-image never lets us look at or enjoy sensations very fully, and, when we do see them clearly, we break the 'little' purposes of the self-image. If we learn to embrace the raw energy of frustration, planning, or discrimination, we can respond to them in a different way. Planning, for instance, could become a source of energy for us, which we could directly investigate and which might yield a glimpse of unexpected vastness.

Every sensation can be discovered to be a vast realm. Usually we slide off the surface of things, not even noticing them before we 'identify' them and become caught up in our habitual responses to them. We can safely give up such identifications; they have nothing to do with insight. We may 'give up' without fearing that we have lost our meditation, that is, we can touch the basic energy of 'identifying' and realize its richness, rather than getting carried away by it. In this way, we can have new relationships with anger, hatred, fear, greed —everything that we usually shut out, cling to, or ignore in our search for 'reality'. These feelings are themselves one side of the Five Wisdoms of reality.

Kum Nye shows that the only reality we need to seek is that given by the 'fact' of every situation. We must firmly grasp this 'fact', for merely sitting quietly and waiting for something to happen is not likely to lead to wisdom. 'Sitting practice' and 'mindfulness' may be just a kind of habit . . . they may not have either deep relaxation or real insight. It is important to penetrate directly to the center of what is going on.

There are two ways of speaking about seizing the opportunity presented by each moment of our existence. The immediacy of each situation seems to be its presence as the moment, so we naturally begin to appreciate it by watching only our present, rather than our past or future (which cannot be found as such). But if we become very familiar with the basic energy of the felt present, we may find that there is no 'present' as such either. Instead, there is only openness, timelessness, only 'happening'.

'Happening' does not mean that 'such and such is coming into being', nor is it really 'beyond time'. 'Nowness' does not refer to something beyond time, but it also does not refer to what we ordinarily see going on 'right now'. It is a more subtle idea than people who say "be in the here and now" may realize. We may have many preliminary 'understandings' when we begin meditation practice, but it is good to realize that these are *our* understandings—they may not yet be broad enough to be generally true. The great masters who used such terms as 'nowness' were beyond 'understanding something'. We need experience, not exciting theories. Here, experience is not something which is 'had' by an ego, a subject. Everything that arises is a center of experience, each thing is 'expressive' and 'appreciative'. It is not our doing or accomplishment. So we can forget about excitedly congratulating ourselves ... we may be very calm and balanced. A calmness like this is very ordinary, very dependable, and serves as the basis for the development of great confidence.

Confidence, in this case, is also not something 'we' have, but a general feature of our situation ... the universe is confident, so to speak. There is no particular state of affairs or reason why this is so. It is a confidence that cannot be shaken because it is not asserted or supported in the first place. Finally, as our practice improves still more, confidence provides the atmosphere for a perception of the freshness and newness of everything. Such perception has no connection with subjects or objects and involves no referring or characterizing. It is a tribute to an essential purity which it also has itself.

A second way of explaining what we need to do in grasping the immediacy of our situation is to talk about 'first instants'. By the 'first instant' of a situation we mean the seldom-noticed stage at which it is possible to grasp the 'fact' of what is arising without naively accepting it as a 'such-and-such'. For a very brief time at the onset of a situation, even at the onset of our sleep and dreams, we can penetrate to the heart of what is happening with relative ease. But if we miss this chance, we fall more and more deeply into a realm of engagements which have no clarity, no lightness—we just get caught up in preoccupations. So depending on how quickly and subtly we can look, the task of embodying new values can be accomplished easily in an instant, or must take a long time as we struggle in the midst of very solid, sticky situations.

There is a Christian saying that we must be constantly ready to enter the door to heaven, for opportunities of entry are rare—the door may open and shut again in a flash, catching us unaware. This is something like that idea. Such techniques as Kum Nye and Shin Jhong help us in the beginning of our practice to counteract the obscuring power of emotions like anger and fear. Eventually, as we become more skillful, they also help us to see the subtle beginning of such manifestations, to welcome them all as expressions of realization. Even the idea of 'moments' may be forgotten. Ordinarily, we talk about past, present, and future as being together, and in terms of our feelings this is true. We feel our present as being connected with our past and future. But if we watch moments closely, we see that they have no 'sides' in relation to any past or future, no way of having temporal 'position'. Without 'past' and 'future', there is no 'present' either . . . not even any separate moments. The tight collection of separate moments which make up our lives can become complete openness and freedom.

The difference between the lightness of 'first instants' and the solid, dark struggles which usually follow is not a matter of the different qualities of certain external circumstances. Rather, it points to a loss of relaxation, attention, and humor on our part. It is we who are clinging to our suffering while refusing to remain in contact with its vital, awakening aspects. Kum Nye begins our training in the art of being very fluid and open in our perceptions and actions. Given 'openness' and receptivity, attention to 'the present' and to 'first instants' becomes the same in practice, because everything is constantly 'coming into being'.

One important consequence of fluidity in thinking and acting is an increase in our tolerance of our fellow human beings. Human relationships often involve very unfair expectations and resentments. These can be overcome by proper meditation practice. By learning to see things more clearly, to recognize the workings of our own self-images, we may accept the 'fact' of other peoples' behavior—that behavior is also the work of their self-images. People are not deliberately spoiling our—and their—chances for happiness. We all share a tendency toward the dimming of awareness and the arising of ignorance. Deep realization of this fact can only inspire compassion, not bitterness.

Essentially, the effect of such practices as Kum Nye is to give us control over our situations and progress. We do not need to depend on anything outside of our own awareness. Dependence on external guides can lead to mistrust, suspicions, surrender of responsibilities, and weakness. Kum Nye emphasizes a kind of self-help, self-massage, which becomes self-healing, self-confidence, and self-realization. This 'self' is not a fixed personality acting in a fixed world, but the presence of reality which nourishes all beings alike. Reality offers us many more possibilities of embodiment than we usually actualize. In a sense, Kum Nye—like all Buddhist practice—is an exercise which we, our world, and our companions are all involved in together and benefit from together.

Shin Jhong

We cannot say very much about Shin Jhong here. Basically, the important thing is to see how it relates to the previous practice of Kum Nye. When we have learned relaxation and balance, and can deeply appreciate our sensations, then Shin Jhong can go further—our awareness can penetrate to more profound and basic levels of reality. Our ordinary awareness is such a limited thing, so controlled by habits. For Shin Jhong, awareness means more like 'light', wisdom, intuition, the seed of enlightenment, self-liberation.

Awareness is vast, not tied down to some specific observer or thing observed. This may sound like a very idealistic position, some fantasy about retreating into mind, away from the world's problems. People often think that birth, struggle, desire, and death are the ordinary events in life, the 'normal'

ones. So these high-sounding ideas about awareness seem very
fantastic and escapist. But maybe they are really not so fantastic—perhaps they are more 'normal' and practical than our
usual preoccupations.

Shin Jhong can lead us back to those levels of awareness
which are very useful and which are like treasure-houses. We
usually attach all our knowledge and memories to the transi-
tory bits and pieces of our ego . . . if we want to remember
something, we have to find the part of the ego that it's tacked
onto. Sometimes the supports for memory have disintegrated
or become lost. But beyond these impermanent structures
there is a vast realm of awareness that preserves everything
perfectly, like a great refrigerator. We can put all the knowledge we want there and retrieve it whenever we like. There is
also much other useful information kept there. In the past,
people became very learned by making use of these deep,
clear levels of mind. They did not try to escape anywhere, but
just took proper advantage of their complete heritage as human beings. Western psychologists still have very little
knowledge of what lies beyond the ordinary mind.

The Human Development Training Programs at the Nyingma Institute are intended to make a bridge between the teachings of the East and West, to bring these deeper kinds of
awareness within the reach of modern psychological investigation. We have done much preliminary 'tasting' in the last
two programs, and I think something very useful will ultimately result. Traditionally much more time than two months
is needed to properly understand all these practices, but even
this time is more than most professional people have to spare.
Still, during these eight-week periods, many peoples' lives
have completely changed. This result has come from just our
beginning work, with discussions of eight consciousnesses,
Kum Nye and Shin Jhong, and analysis of the various manifestations of mind.

The different papers published in this book are a few of the projects undertaken by participants in the Human Development Training Programs. In the future we may explore more advanced subjects and publish papers which consider meditative techniques in more detail. Many lifetimes of good work and research remain to be done. I invite all those who have something to contribute to this exciting job to come and help us.

Western Psychology Meets Tibetan Buddhism

Gay Gaer Luce

Anyone who arrived at 1815 Highland Place two days before the official opening of the Nyingma Institute would have seen roofers, painters, carpenters, and upholsterers busy at work, and debris piled high in the parking lot—in short, a catastrophe. The Padma Ling students, with a few volunteers, had worked around the clock. On June 24th, the arriving "students" found clean if spartan quarters, and were a little surprised to be handed brooms and mops. This was not the smoothly staffed American institution they were used to; in-

GAY GAER LUCE is a graduate of Stanford and Radcliff, and holds a Ph.D. in psychology from Union Graduate School. A three-time winner of the American Psychological Foundation's Science Award, she is founder and director of Senior Actualization and Growth Explorations (SAGE); her book *Body Time* contributed to changing long-accepted concepts of aging and fatigue. After graduating from the 1973 Human Development Training Program, she taught Kum Nye classes and special programs at the Nyingma Institute.

stead, they were expected to help keep the place clean, clear the garden of broken glass, and help prepare or clean up after meals. Our very arrival was an immediate lesson in the Buddhist secret of survival, a philosophy which urges the acceptance of life as it is, rather than an effort to meet expectations. The Institute was the opposite of all that is institutional: nobody could be a passive recipient of food, lodging, and instruction without becoming part of a community. Similarly, the instruction was often socratic, involving direct experience and very little book work.

During the summer training program, we spent seven or eight hours together in class, with assigned practices that should have absorbed another four hours—a full day. From 8 A.M. to 5 P.M. we sat on folded pillows in an incense-fragrant room, the lama seated before us on a raised platform, relaxed, and informally talking in a manner that was deceptively simple. He asked a few questions. "What is the difference between calmness and stillness? . . . What is sound?" We gave the articulate answers one might expect of educated professionals: "Sound is the pressure of air waves on the eardrum, a physiological response, a pattern of neuronal activity, etc." But as we listened to ourselves we began to get the message: what we accept for answers is simply the reduction of one concept or construct to another. We knew little about the experience of sound—although we were sitting in a relatively noisy room, over a street with some traffic. Noise, as Rinpoche observed, is a problem in America which can be destructive and create tension and disturbed thoughts. But there are many ways to experience sound. For instance, we were asked to become the sound, putting our entire consciousness into it. Then he asked us to see with our ears, listen with our eyes. This exercise was calculated to make one realize how much conscious control we can exert over sensory functions that seem fixed and involuntary. Actually one can alter the habit of hearing so that sounds produce images of bodily sensations.

This first week it was difficult to sit still and watch our

experience. We were discovering how heavily we had come to rely on words and constructs, experiencing the world in terms of discriminations and differences. Western education fosters a dualistic mode of thinking, and we tend to focus first on what is external to ourselves, learning to drive a car before we have learned to control our minds. To sit quietly for five minutes without entertaining a thought or image is not so easy.

We may have imagined we were relaxed, but we had yet to learn physical and mental relaxation before we could start to concentrate. "Deep relaxation can alter all of living," Rinpoche said. "When you are tight you cannot feel. Go deep. There is calmness and understanding there . . . satisfaction. Others cannot always please us, but in meditation we can learn to please ourselves." To relax, he taught us uniquely Tibetan forms of self-massage of the face, neck and upper body, using strong pressures, verging on painful. Many of the relaxation exercises were familiar: breathing in unison, listening to one's heartbeat, or chanting. Ironically, instead of bliss, some of us were now aware of muscle tensions we hadn't noticed before, inhibited feelings that crept out in tears, and the unruly noisiness of our minds, which kept up a kind of ceaseless chatter whenever we tried to be still.

Rinpoche offered special practices for physical relaxation and concentration to help us diminish the conversation in our heads. Sometimes we visualized complex images in dynamic interaction. Vajrayāna Buddhism relies heavily upon visualization, a method that is alien to most of our academic training. Generally, it is assumed that eidetic imagery vanishes when children reach about age eight, yet Rinpoche can glance at a painting, and later close his eyes and see it in detail. Many artists cannot do this. As a Stanford University design professor has complained, many engineering and architecture students cannot visualize. "They can talk about it, not see it or draw it." Perhaps because we rely so heavily on language, we cultivate the functions of our left hemisphere at the neglect of the right. Thinking themselves "non-visual," many people accept this label as a physiological axiom rather than a habit. Our culture fosters a kind of snobbish self-approval in the articulate person, despite the fact that language is linear and inadequate to express complicated concepts. Einstein and other creative scientists have often mentioned the need to think in images.

Visualizing, like learning tennis, merely takes practice and energy. However, it was easier for me to follow a tennis teacher who insisted I practice a serve, than to be told I must spend six hours gazing at a white Tibetan letter on a black background. I remember worrying that it would be six long hours of fruitless boredom. Physical action and small rewards keep one going in a sport, but in practicing mental functions, many many hours of inaction may pass before there is the incredible joy of really seeing that image, three-dimensional and bright, hanging in the blackness. One should be able to see any image, at will, and hold it for long periods of time without interference from thoughts or sense perceptions. This is just a first step in learning to meditate, and it seemed an impossibility to many of us.

Unused to sitting cross-legged on the floor, quite a few people found themselves distracted by painful ankles, lower back aches, unwanted itches, and extremities tingling with poor circulation. A few people gave up the posture and sat in chairs or leaned against walls and pillars. Rinpoche seemed to sense our discomfort and usually followed a period of physical stillness with stretching exercises that he often initiated without announcement by making the movements himself.

Never having taught large groups in a Western manner, Rinpoche was sometimes hard to see and follow, for he did not always repeat himself or explain. Suddenly, during a tea break he would have the entire group picking glass fragments out of the parched earth behind the house. This abruptness, characteristic of religious schools in the Near and Far East, keeps students on the alert. A Chilean-born psychiatrist and teacher who has written extensively on the progression from

psychotherapy to spiritual quest (*The One Quest*), Claudio
Naranjo studied Rinpoche's teaching style with deep interest.
"He always talked at different levels. I would think he was
talking directly to my needs, but he made everyone in the
room feel that he was the center. . . . ."

Most of the participants had taught, or lectured to large
audiences, but Rinpoche had a way of putting us on the spot
so that our pose of confidence was stripped away. He would
pick out someone hiding in the back and ask a direct question.
Or he created games. "Describe meditation in three words,"
he demanded. "But no word repeated." If the fortieth person
repeated, Rinpoche remembered and jumped on him with
glee. "Tranquility is used!" Without warning he would begin a
new topic, beckoning a volunteer to come and stand before
him, and then begin kneading his sternum with a thumb.

A kind of therapy similar to that developed by Wilhelm
Reich is just now beginning to come into use. Vigorous and
demanding physical exercises for cathartic effect or to awaken
new states of mind have been well-known to the Tibetans for
close to 1,400 years. One of the newer therapies, bioenergetics,
consists of exercises developed by one of Reich's students,
Alexander Lowen. These are, like many Tibetan practices,
vocal and sometimes painful. Roughly speaking, they are designed to release blocked emotional energies that have been
frozen into lifelong body postures, as anxiety is sometimes
held in a tightly indrawn stomach. One similar exercise we
used during the summer—the Vajra Āsana—required us to
stand in a very difficult position for five to ten minutes.

Within twenty seconds, knee and thigh pain began. Soon
the body started to tremble. As the pain grew stronger, it was
tempting to rest, but Rinpoche was omnipresent, stop-watch
in hand, glaring at whoever was ready to give up. In a minute
and a half the pain seemed unendurable, and in reaction
many of us found ourselves angry, frustrated, almost sobbing
with self pity. Five minutes seems an eternity the first time.
After two minutes we began chanting "Om"—a choral groan

of agony. Yet, somehow the unendurable became bearable. When the time was up, we lay down for 30 minutes panting in relief. "Control your breathing," we were told. Soon, as in a cold shower after a sauna, we went from a deep catharsis into peace and then into an experience of being energized from every cell.

In bioenergetics, and other Western therapies, stressors are used to unblock emotional energy, but Tibetans go a step beyond catharsis. All emotions, positive or negative, are considered forms of a basic energy. A stress position is merely a way of evoking frustration and pain, to be transformed into pure energy and then used in intensifying a visualization, or to lift a person out of a depressed or hostile mood.

One Texas school teacher in our midst would do such exercises for a half hour as a stimulant when he felt sluggish, but few others did them on their own. We are lazy, as Rinpoche remarked. Moreover, most of us have learned to dread pain, and we create even more distress in our avoidance. It is possible to concentrate on pain unemotionally, with detachment. At that point it turns into pure sensation, a form of energy, a plausible method for enhancing mental vitality.

These Tibetan exercises cannot be considered as medical or psychiatric devices apart from the philosophy in which they evolved. They were not intended to be simply means of handling particular situations. They are integrated into a whole view of life—one that has little sentimentality about death, pain, dirt, or human nastiness. These are not avoided, but seen and accepted. Enlightenment is said to be the ability to live with reality as it is, which means that one must peel away the culture's veneer over the nature of survival or life's brevity. Tibetan prayer beads, used as a kind of rosary, often contain a bead of human bone to remind the adept that all things, including himself, are transient.

This philosophy requires strength and self-mastery, which have never been considered explicit aims of Western schools, nor the antidote for emotional and psychosomatic illness.

Buddhist therapy assumes that the person to be helped must
have or acquire an unembellished view of reality, and that
self-transcendence is the path toward health. Although some
of the new therapies (Psychosynthesis, Transpersonal therapy,
Biofeedback, etc.) take this view, Western medicine is predom-
inantly oriented around treating problems, such as a symptom, drug abuse, depression, phobias. "What I mainly learned
here," remarked one psychologist, "was how limited my concept of therapy has been. Ninety percent of what we are
concerned with would be a joke to Rinpoche." The Western
therapist would try to help his patient with the so-called presenting problem, were it a migraine headache, fear of darkness, or a poor marriage. The symptom might be seen as the
first of a string of problems that could be traced back to
childhood. A Buddhist might see no problem at all, except in
the person's current expectations and attitudes. Americans,
particularly, feel that life is abnormal when it is not happy and
smooth, but Buddhists accept that suffering is part of the
human condition. Rinpoche convinced at least a few of the
participants that Western psychotherapy, and particularly
analysis, may create more problems than it solves. Many
children, and adults, blame their parents for defects that Tibetans assume to be the inevitable flaws of the human condition. Psychotherapies often encourage this retrospective anger
by magnifying past deprivations and focusing upon defects in
parent-child relationships.

Like most Asians, Tibetans revere their elders and maintain family harmony even at some cost to the individuals.
From Rinpoche's eyes we Americans are restlessly mobile.
We express so much dissatisfaction with our country, that we
seem to be unaware—as he sees it—that we live in a golden age
of affluence and religious freedom. Appreciate it and enjoy
this rarity in earth's history, he kept saying. But our family life
puzzled him. There seemed to be so much disharmony, and
the nuclear family without room for the aged seemed cruel.
One of the most compelling themes of the entire summer was

compassion. Sensing that we were frequently cut off from feeling, or that we tended to hide behind professionalism, Rinpoche gave exercises such as asking us to recall our earliest childhood and the way our parents nurtured us—feeding, bathing, and nursing us at the helpless stage of infancy. How could we possibly repay them for giving us life? Instead of blaming parents for present dissatisfactions, he urged, we should try to visualize their sufferings, their impoverished or neglected lives, and especially feel the loneliness of old people, so fragile and overlooked.

Although nobody could be untouched by Rinpoche's own depth of compassion, many of the psychotherapists insisted that they had to deal with their patients' problems in Western terms. By the end of the summer, a few had changed. Aubrey Lindgren, who learned Gestalt from the late Fritz Perls, said, "I've been a problem-oriented therapist for the last eight years, with drug addicts and people who are considered the victims of the world. Now I don't see myself working with their problems—I would rather help them appreciate the remarkable fact of being alive, and have a more serene existence regardless of their circumstances." Every few days, Rinpoche, with a mischievous gleam, would bait us to demonstrate how we, the professional experts, went about helping people. "I have a problem," he would announce, grinning broadly. "I don't believe in myself—how would you help me?" It was a losing game to answer professionally. We were not ready to ask what lies behind self-belief; indeed, what is the concept of self? Insofar as the lama could see, the theories underlying our professionalism were hopelessly fragmentary and confused, like Freud's Oedipal theory.

It was inevitable that we should come to a hilarious confrontation over Freud, and American sexual hangups that were unheard of in Tibet. "Why do you not relax?" he would ask, regarding sex. "When you have big expectations, you cannot feel." Our high expectations caused tensions that prevented pure sexual experience and enjoyment—and psuedo-

medical manifestos demanding orgasm were at fault with the
rest of the culture. Our culture overloads sex with so many
associations—prestige, money, emotional needs (dependency,
ascendency, etc.), along with irrelevancies built up by ads, TV,
and movies—that few people have plain, unalloyed sexual
experience. As we tried to reach an understanding about
basic sexuality in discussing Freudian theory, Rinpoche
commented that Freud, a product of Western sexual confusion, could never have intended to say that children were
sexually attracted to their parents. Therapists in the group
wagged their heads, referred to cases, and heartily disagreed.
But Rinpoche was emphatic. "Impossible!" he said. He was so
emphatic that it prompted one young man to assert that he
was attracted not only to his mother, but his father as well.
Rinpoche was totally dumbfounded. "To your parents?" he
asked, incredulous. When the laughter died down, it was clear
that he referred to a basic physical drive, and purely physical
attraction. To us, sexual attraction meant those many nuances
and associations that might lead to sexual thoughts or inter-
course. He meant sex. We were talking about S*e*x.

We were not yet capable of teasing apart the many elements of our experience, to see what aspects were based on
concepts, conditioned emotions, or accidental associations. It
was not until much later that our mental exercises began to
give us the tools we needed to analyze our own experience. We
may have been professionals at verbal analysis, but in the land
of interior feeling, we were fumbling.

At the bottom of a great deal of violence and sickness is the
inability to handle emotions. In extremes, for instance, it
shows up in the fact that over 600,000 U.S. children are bru-
talized every year, usually by parents who have no idea that
there is any way of controlling the emotions they feel. The
same might be said of the more than 50,000 people who die
(directly or indirectly) because of alcohol each year. All summer we practiced different exercises that would help us (and
also patients or students) to master negative feelings. While

most of them would make poor reading, they worked. For instance, after an enraging or frustrating event, one could stop long enough to inspect one's behavior, and ask, Am *I* that rage? "Make a model of the feeling," Rinpoche said, "so you can cook it, boil it, eat it." Sometimes we meditated on a negative emotion at the time it happened, trying to see it with a relaxed mind, free of concepts, watching the energy. Several people were surprised to realize how much they enjoyed their anger, and how little they really wanted to change. The architect in our midst said he would look at negative feelings until they became neutral. By the end of the summer he felt he was no longer controlled by his feelings, but that he had the control: "I don't have to waste my energy jumping into emotional situations and reacting negatively."

Detachment, a central concept in Buddhism, is largely misunderstood in the West. It is not detachment from life, but from the conditioned hangups we consider normal. We accept competition, avarice, and deceit as normal in personal and economic life, yet strangely enough we never consider that they have consequences for health. Therapists must treat individuals who live in a world of Watergate and corporate connivance, yet traditionally we consider health beyond the domain of morality. Thus in the Buddhist view, we can never go to the source of our problems, be they drug addiction, alcoholism, or neurosis. One can see how moral conflicts could create illness. In the so-called socialization process, a child is encouraged to utter small lies. At first the falsity may be accompanied by a felt tension. After many repetitions, it may become subliminal. Finally, in adulthood, the person may catch his breath before speaking, and suffer from the respiratory ailments of shallow breathers. The consequences of one's actions are expressed in the idea of *karma*, a word that is used faddishly today, but which implies the principle that good begets good, and evil, evil. Because of our cultural conditioning, however, we no longer see these chains of action and reaction in our lives.

All summer Rinpoche gave us simple, straight-forward exercises in reversing stereotyped habits. These showed us how our most inconspicuous habits were affecting us. "Don't say 'yes' for a week," he instructed. This makes embarrassingly clear the amount of time and energy spent daily on hypocrisy, assenting to be nice, or from habit. He asked us to be silent for a weekend. We create friction and dissipate our energies in needless talk. Silence can heal agitated patients, he said, and periods of silence at meals or during the evening might be an emollient to disharmonious families. For example, paying attention to posture or sitting, or using the left hand if one is right handed, all stimulate one to the kind of mindfulness that is essential to Buddhist development. As one begins to notice how many aspects of one's character, posture, body vitality and mental habits there are to watch, then it is plain why enlightenment is considered the job of a lifetime, or perhaps many lifetimes.

Along with a vast number of simple, and direct exercises that would show us to ourselves—like looking into a mirror—if we took the trouble to do them, there were several meditations on which Rinpoche placed particular emphasis. One required our concentrating single-pointedly at the reflection of our eyes in a mirror for three hours at a stretch, or until we had done it for twenty-four hours.

A garbage truck was grinding outside our dimly lit classroom, and I recall looking around at the dismayed faces, as Rinpoche added this assignment. Some of the local participants were still holding office hours for patients, or had prior commitments for evenings. It was getting to be a choice between homework and sleep. In Tibet, a student fortunate enough to hear his teaching would have followed Rinpoche's instructions to the letter whatever the cost. But we had not completed our twenty-four hours by the end of the week. Rinpoche was beginning to see that our commitment to learning was not undivided, and that we were busy even when we considered ourselves to be free. If he was privately perplexed or disappointed, he adroitly turned unaccomplished written assignments into group discussions. We could not fully appreciate the uniqueness of our curriculum: it was so condensed that we were to attempt, in twenty-four hours, what a Tibetan might have done for six months. Still, six hours of meditation in a day seemed infinite to me.

I sat before the mirror, expecting nothing, watching my monkey face watch me. I had envied others who saw visions, experienced telepathy, or other psychic phenomena, or easily entered deep hypnotic trances. My scientific skepticism, perhaps, had kept me so anchored to earth that I doubted I would ever enjoy the magical or transcendent experiences others seemed to enter so easily. Suddenly, the face I had believed to be my own looked at me with an expression so alien and inhuman that I gasped audibly. When the fear abated, I saw that the face was quite old, wizened. It looked dead. Suddenly it became a child looking at me with candid curiosity. Faces came toward me in a procession, some of them familiar, my mother, an uncle, a Mongol with cruel features, a medieval abbess, a catlike Burmese, my death-mask, people who might have been the grandparents I had never known, and among them a dark brown chimpanzee. I watched, not conscious of any emotion, and at some point the mirror darkened and went black. My eyes were open but I saw nothing! This, as I later learned, was a common experience when people truly quieted their minds. It did not last. In a few seconds, the procession of faces resumed, and at some point a region between the eyes began to sparkle like a strobe. Then, perhaps in surprise, or fear, I felt disoriented in space, as if I were falling. I was . . . my face touched the mirror.

Each of us had projected our own fear, self-disapproval or infatuation, anger, or some other distortion onto the image in the mirror, projections that we saw visually. However, when we achieved a state of emptiness, without thoughts and projections, the images—including that of our own face—would vanish.

Rinpoche listened benignly, drawing out some reticent or shy members, pointedly leaving others alone. He had an uncanny way of knowing where we were at, even if we didn't speak. On a grey morning, he would sometimes make a motion in the air as if to cut the fog in our heads. He would abruptly have us stand. "Bend and touch the floor," he commanded. "Bend back. Now close your eyes. What color do you see?" He went around the room. People certainly saw different parts of the spectrum. Most of us would have dismissed a splash of color in our visual field as not worth noting. But Rinpoche was interested. From these traces he seemed to be measuring something about our consciousness, as if it were familiar territory. It was awesome to realize that a Tibetan teacher would understand the private signs of inner events as though they were written on a map. Nothing was dismissed. A color, a sensation, was significant: it told where our minds were in their evolution to greater refinement.

In response to his question about color, one man who had been sitting skeptically in the back replied, "Blue." "Ah, blue. The color of Buddhahood, serenity," Rinpoche remarked, quickly adding, "and also of ignorance, stupidity." Self-congratulation was punctured as fast as it arose, and competing for praise was a self-defeating effort. The moment a person perfected a yoga position, Rinpoche would praise and push in the same sentence. "That's very good—now hold it for two minutes," he would say as the person gasped to his limit. Every day we added to our repertoire of Tibetan Yoga positions, some of which resembled isometrics. While some of these were unfamiliar, they had the familiar purpose of enhancing mental and physical awareness, improving muscle tone, and balance and concentration.

Rinpoche's instruction in diagnosis involved sitting in front of a person in a state of emptiness, observing without words or barriers everything about them. Professional questionnaires and scientific evaluations are often a substitute for close observation, a skill that is rarely explicitly trained even in medical schools. Moreover, it is a skill that would be useless without emptying the mind, for our ceaseless mental activity, biases, and preconceptions would filter out important information. Even when we think ourselves quiet, there is some mental noise occluding perception. Anyone who wants to see this for himself can perform a test that Rinpoche gave. He said, "Count all your thoughts for an hour." This meant all thoughts, images, sensations, sounds, feelings—anything you are aware of. (My own count was over a thousand.)

Some breathing exercises we were introduced to are practiced to open up crucial nodes, known as *cakra*s. According to the yoga teachings of the Near and Far East since about the sixth century century B.C., and the theory of acupuncturists, the center of energy is the cerebrospinal axis of the spinal column and brain. The *cakra*s correspond roughly to nerve foci that control body functioning and the endocrine system. At the base of the spine is the *cakra* of reproductive energy, the famous kundalini energy. The aim of many exercises is to release this energy toward the *cakra*s of the solar plexus, the heart, throat, third eye, and crown. Without knowing it, most people have seen designs of the *cakra* system in the central geometrics of oriental rugs. Many Christian saints in the brass reliefs of the eleventh and twelfth centuries have a diamond or other design on the forehead between the eyebrows at the point known as the *cakra* of superconsciousness, or psychic center. In addition to representing centers for internal functioning, the *cakra*s also represent receivers for cosmic energies and geomagnetic changes. We were hoping that our breathing exercise would allow us to channel energy, open spinal *cakra*s, and perhaps remove our blocks to higher awareness.

In actuality, the first breathing sessions sounded more like a ward of gasping emphysemics. Rinpoche, calmly seated with his colorful striped quilt over his legs, told us to take off sweaters, despite the dampness and chill in the room.

With repetition of the exercise, the nature of the experience changed. A man reported an opening in the region of his heart. A few people felt energy crawling up the spine, and found their heads filled with brilliant light. Claudio Naranjo said, "This is a most important exercise for me. I had the sensation of being born anew into many states of consciousness I never experienced before." Yet he confessed that he feared for his life each breath, positive he would never make it back alive. I, too, felt that fear, despite a peculiar tranquility as if my body were a mere anchor. One of the problems of unsupervised practice of these breathing exercises is that people can unwittingly do themselves damage, and incite startling changes in consciousness that they cannot handle alone.

We began almost every afternoon with chanting, creating a human ocean of sound that can arouse strangely primordial feelings. Americans, Rinpoche noticed, seemed particularly susceptible to chanting, which could rapidly create fellow-feeling, or a transition from ordinary conversation to the stillness of meditation.

Ability to meditate varied in the group. My own, still at the neanderthal level, often left me wishing I could stop thoughts, sneeze without disturbing the group, scratch or conquer numbness and pain in my legs. If the ache and thoughts evaporated for a few moments, I would be so overjoyed and proud of my momentary stillness that I would end it with what the Buddhists call grasping. The paradox of meditation, like relaxation, is that one must maintain it without making an effort. My efforts not to make an effort usually plunged me into a yet more primitive state—drowsiness. Prior to this course I might have described myself as energetic, but profound laziness began to show itself as we proceeded to the more demanding meditations.

Analytical meditation was one of the basic tools for self-understanding, by directly inspecting the nature of inner experience without words or metaphors. If we heard a sound we were to begin by inquiring, "Who heard the sound?" and to look within for the hearing part of ourselves. Then we were to ask, "Who is looking at he who hears?" and "Who is observing the observer?" None of this questioning was intellectual but wordless. For many people it became a regression, as endless as a hall of mirrors. Some responded with a characteristic violence, seeing their past self-images with pain and longing to escape, feeling as though they were burning. The products of this kind of inward look are undramatic, but they were substantial for each person. An articulate Italian professor discovered that his so-called random thoughts were not random: they were the cravings of different parts of himself, and he could trace the origins of each "random" thought in this meditation.

A few people found that the procedure led to a loss of their sense of identity, extremely frightening for a Westerner, although it is desirable in Buddhist development. We had begun to ask questions about our own nature that we had probably not asked since adolescence, the questions of children before they are frustrated and turned off by cultural indifference. Who am I? *Where* is the entity called a self? Is it possible I don't exist—that there is only an awareness encrusted by concepts of self and ego? Is it possible that this awareness could function in its body without any need for a personality?

During our first meetings, Rinpoche had innocently asked, "What is a thought?" Our replies had come from books and teachers, external responses that would not be considered knowledge by a Buddhist, for knowledge must be felt. By mid-July we were beginning to analyze a thought by a mapping that is uniquely Nyingma, a system that has been validated over the centuries.

In the momentary blankness between thoughts, which appears to be so fleeting to us, the Nyingma lamas have mapped at least nine discrete conscious states. Like the Eskimos with their more than twenty words for snow, these nuances of experience have inspired a sizable vocabulary and take very fine tuning to detect. Needless to say, this interior cartography cannot be taught by books, but requires the guidance and feedback of a teacher.

The ground state between thoughts, ever present in varying density, has been called *kun-gzhi*. Like gravity, it has many gradations and may be experienced as heavier or lighter, but so long as one remains in an earthly consciousness, it is present. The heavier *kun-gzhi* is a densely peaceful state, experienced briefly by athletes after a maximum exertion, a blankness experienced after deep breathing exercises or orgasm. It resembles inebriation, and it could, indeed, be used to help an alcoholic or drug-addicted person, since it is a state they seek. For instance by running up and down hill for 25 minutes, or doing a strenuous exercise, they could perhaps be taught to induce this state. Once having learned the feeling, they could be taught how to attain and perpetuate the serenity without drugs.

We would do an exercise to induce the oceanic blankness of *kun-gzhi*, and then like fishermen awaiting a nibble, we would await a flicker of energy, a distant harbinger of a movement that could become a thought in the back of the head. It might stir like a barely perceived breeze or light, a distant restlessness that was called *kun-gzhi rnam-shes*. Soon after, one might feel a sense of identification as if the perception were one's own, a subtle discrimination—a state labeled as *nyon-yid*.

We were beginning to inspect the processes that Westerners call the unconscious. In many of our exercises we had been getting ready to train our sight on the terrain that is a forbidden no-man's-land according to Western psychology. The conscious mind does not sit and stare at the workings of the unconscious, according to post-Freudian understanding. Yet we were doing precisely this. The presumption that a part of our consciousness is inaccessible—is unconscious—may be based mainly on Western habits. We rarely sit still and observe our minds. Moreover, we have nobody to teach us how to watch our processes. Mental events seem mercurial and too rapid to watch in ordinary consciousness. It had taken us many weeks of intensive daily training before we could slow down our thoughts enough, and sharpen our awareness so that we could begin to observe and identify the many kinds of events between one thought and another—watching the "unconscious" at work.

Tibetan Buddhist theory, which is comprehensive beyond our expectations of a psychological theory, depends upon much direct observation, and presumes extensive mental training. Tibetans have a metaphor for the untrained mind: a one-armed rider on a blind wild horse.

The rampant quality of that restless, untrained mind is evident in our pathology, and in our relative neglect of introspection. In the last ten years, a few Western scientists like Dr. Joe Kamiya, in San Francisco, or Dr. Elmer Green, at The Menninger Foundation, have been trying to correlate inner experience with EEG (Electroencephalogram) tracings, in order to construct a matrix and vocabulary for introspective experience. EEG is a limited instrument (because of the limits of the machines of the 1930s, we study only the brainwave frequencies between 1–50 CPS, although there are brainwave changes occurring in thousands of cycles per second); nonetheless it may be fruitful to match the subtle Tibetan mapping with EEG tracings—once a scientist interested in this problem has himself learned the Tibetan cartography of consciousness. To be given a glimpse of a well-developed inner language and technique for watching the "unconscious" is extraordinary enough, but in addition we were given access to sleep and dreaming in a way that is also beyond the inquiry of the waking mind.

Most of our emotional associations are created haphazardly, and, for the most part, we do not know why we react to a particular color. Indeed, we usually don't know what aspects of our environment trigger our feelings. It became apparent that the boundaries between one's self and the outside world depends on our conscious habits of maintaining fixed perception patterns. Throughout the summer we had cultivated certain images in order to construct deliberate associations and desired emotional states that could be produced at will.

There were certainly personal changes during the eight-week summer session: a physician, Michael Smith, spoke for many when he observed that he had become more patient and able to concentrate. Several people felt they had accomplished what therapy or prior psychoanalysis had failed to do—gaining control over their emotions and discovering that they had a choice of how they would react. Many people expressed greater ease and tranquility as a result. (One woman emphasized that her tranquility was not fragile, but that she remained serene even in the midst of a family crisis in which her mother had nearly died.) During the summer we had occasionally stopped to assay changes in consciousness. Some people were sleeping less. Others were noticing a sensory brilliance, as if the world were suffused with the clear colors of childhood, and a return to sensory innocence. One social worker from New Jersey remarked that he had tested his consciousness by trying to flip a coin and predict the outcome. With eyes closed he flipped, and guessed correctly the first time. He tried again, and again he was right. After being right nine times in a row he quit. Rinpoche was much amused. "Maybe he should go to the racetrack," he said.

Some of the effects which required the cloistered intensity of the training period, might have been attributed to the lack of noise and busyness of everyday life, but two months later, lives were changing. Claudio Naranjo found himself thrust into a period of solitary work, a retreat. Reverend Tilden Edwards of the Episcopal Diocese in Washington, D.C. was ebullient with a new inner freedom and deepened sense of compassion. He is Director of the Ecumenical Training Center in Washington, and since his return he has found himself leaning less heavily on behavioral science for therapy, and more on meditation. Following the Buddhist program, which ended in late August, Rev. Edwards went to a week-long Jesuit retreat. His understanding of the Christian saints had deepened. "I often found myself thinking, that is just what Rinpoche told us, as I read them: now I feel I can express and share their religious experience far more deeply." At the level of deep mystical experience there is really not much difference between the Christian and the Buddhist saint, but direct experience is precisely what has been missing from most of the Christian churches for many years, and this is where meditation training may have a considerable impact in reviving religious experience.

People look for external changes. Professor Donald Michael seemed lighter to his friends, who told him that he had lost weight, which he hadn't—at least not physical weight. He found that he was looking at his life in new perspective, and that it was becoming lighter, less complicated. "I find myself simplifying," he said. "For instance, by October I usually have 10–15 speaking engagements lined up. But I began asking myself why I was speaking." Prestige, importance, he decided, no longer interested him. Speaking engagements and endless committees used to complicate his life. "I do ask myself whether I'm copping out, whether I am judging the value of things correctly . . . but even that question has more meaning now. I never enjoyed cognitive thinking so much before."

Many students felt that the most important experience of the eight weeks was Rinpoche himself. "He represents a different ideal of what a fully realized human being can become." He has qualities of rootedness, a childlike joy and curiosity, and a kind of cosmic noblesse oblige. Rinpoche's profound mastery and knowledge of the use of psychic energies gave him an awesome quality, and we were aware of the immensity and unfamiliarity of his universe.

Everyone knew that in eight weeks we would only scratch the surface of the Nyingma psychology. Today it is painfully clear that there is only one way of learning the comprehensive psychological skills—it is essential to have a guide. Only by deeply studying with the lamas of the Nyingma tradition will we ever have a glimmering idea of the scope of their work.

Verily, there is a realm where there is neither the solid nor the fluid, neither heat nor motion, neither this world nor any other world, neither sun nor moon. . . . There is, O monks, an Unborn, Unoriginated, Uncreated, Unformed. If there were not this Unborn, this Unoriginated, this Uncreated, this Unformed, escape from the world of the born, the originated, the created, the formed, would not be possible.[1]

—Śākyamuni Buddha

Although the One Mind is, it has no existence. Being the source of all the bliss of Nirvāṇa and of all the sorrow of the Sangsāra, it is cherished like the Eleven Yānas.[2]

—Padmasambhava

As it does not occur to a man whom a magician has conjured up (when he looks at the audience): 'I will please those people,' and nevertheless he performs his work; they see him exhibiting manifold illusory works, although he has no body, thought or name. Just so it never occurs to one who courses in wisdom: 'Having known enlightenment I will set free the world!' In his various rebirths he is associated with manifold works, which he manifests like magical illusions, but he does not course in false discrimination.[3]

—Śākyamuni Buddha

Vanishing Magician-Spectator, Rabbit, and Hat

Claudio Naranjo

What is mind? Mind asks the question and mind knows the answer. And it is mind, too, that creates within itself an opacity that separates the questioner from the answerer, the subject from the object of knowing. As the one or the other, mind approximately coincides with "us," as when we conceive of our-selves as a mind inhabiting a body—but do we ever experience our "selves"? It is more exact to say that the conception of ourselves is a product of the mind, too, and that the mind transcends self-idea and self-image. These are thoughts

CLAUDIO NARANJO, M.D., has studied at Harvard and the University of Illinois on a Fulbright Scholarship and in 1966 went to the University of California, Berkeley, on a Guggenheim Fellowship. A practicing psychiatrist, he was a major figure in the early years of Esalen Institute and later founded SAT, a nation-wide group for personal growth. His works include *The One Quest, On the Psychology of Meditation, The Healing Journey,* and various papers on Gestalt therapy.

that take form in the mental matrix and float in it along with other thoughts. As subject or as object, "I" is a mental event, a mental state, or a construct. Could it be that "mind" itself is another construct, a hypothetical entity with the power of manifesting our experience, that we have taken for reality and in a sense reified? If there is no magician to cause the rabbits to appear out of the hat, this does not necessarily deny the magical operation. But it would amount to conceiving that there is a dream without a dreamer (except as content of the dream itself). One thing we know, however: magician or not, there is a hat—a black hat from which "we" emerge as a mosaic of mental contents. If the rabbit is real, the hat is just as real. In other words: there is within the province of our experience both a domain of content and a contentless domain. We may think of the two as figure and ground and regard the latter as a field in which mental phenomena crystallize or a substance out of which they are molded into particular form and quality.

From the perspective of the rabbit mind (which in the Buddhist perspective is equated with the samsaric condition) it is the best possible fate to exist as a rabbit, and the hat seems a dangerous darkness, a hole with the appearance of a potentially devouring womb. From the Buddhist perspective (which is, as it were, the perspective of the womb-hat) rabbit life is full of suffering and is rooted in more than unnecessary craving. As an alternative, it is possible to cross to the other shore of rabbit-nature by returning to the hat from which we come, which is nirvana—the dissolution of the magician's illusion. This accomplished—having become, so to say, our egg, our primordial non-form, our original face—it may be possible to come back to rabbit-form and rabbit land for the "Hell" of it (in both senses of the term and in a third as well). This third sense (different from pleasure and pain) is what is called Bodhisattvahood, which is the full accomplishment of Buddhahood manifesting as non-attachment to Buddhahood and as the consequent position of balance between form and formlessness, differentiation and fusion, the world of dream and that of wakefulness.

Our ordinary perspective is one in which we inhabit an island-world of mental contents surrounded by what seems to be nothing. Buddhism, perhaps more insistently and articulately than any other doctrine, tells us that nothing is, more exactly, Nothing, which is, in a sense, something; and even more: Something (the significance of everything). It says: if you plunge into that hat you will at first be afraid of the dark or bored, but then you will see a light which is the essence of your rabbit nature and is your true nature. At first you can only see that light in the dark, but after you have gone in and out of the hat many times you start carrying your hat around with you, and it is like carrying your light-giving dark womb around you in the light of day.

The two domains that I have compared to hat and rabbit, the formless and prearticulate and the formalized or articulate, the nirvanic and the samsaric, exist simultaneously in us. That is why it may be said at the same time both that Buddhahood is our essence and that we are unenlightened, fettered by karma and its residues, unawakened to our true nature. Yet we are samsara-conscious and Buddha-unconscious, more conscious of our ego than our Buddha-nature: only with enlightenment may our consciousness transcend its dependence on words, sensations, feelings, and thoughts, since what was unconscious will then become conscious and we may learn not only to dissolve into emptiness (as in the practice of meditation), but to move in a fluid domain rather than being bound to walking on the solid ground of our island. For the outer domain of manifest content can become increasingly responsive to the inner domain of fluidity or fusion. And to some extent it always is. We may say that the calm and quiet core of our being contains in seed form that which the surface mind spells out or translates in categories of space-time and quality, thus bringing it forth and into full bloom. This is what the Mahayanic doctrine affirms of the eighth and highest

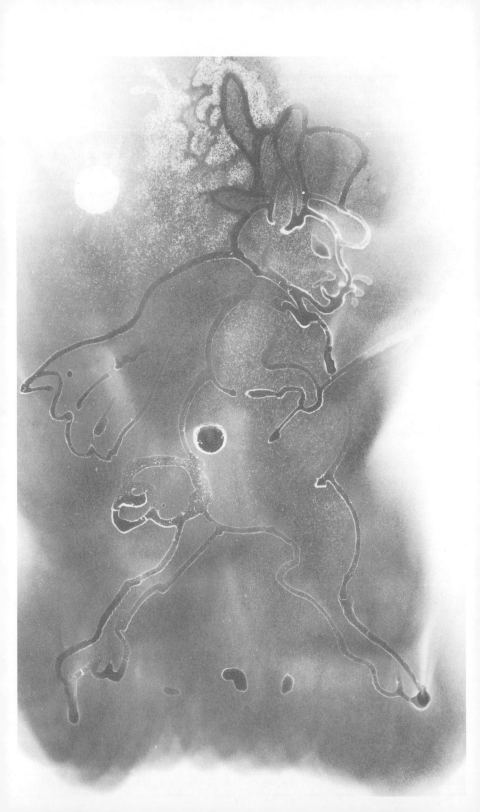

consciousness, the *ālaya* or store-consciousness. *Ālaya* lies beyond the five sense-consciousnesses, beyond the sixth, the conceptual consciousness, and beyond a seventh, the root of ego (the *manas*, which projects a notion of self and a self-identity on the *ālaya*, thus misinterpreting it). Therefore we may say that mental events in the periphery of the mind are selected from the potentiality of the *ālaya* or fundamental consciousness according to conditioned biases of acceptance and rejection. As such, these mental formations are like the shapes that we see in the clouds—also a selection among the multiple possibilities of vision. According to this perspective, Buddhism regards such mental events (*dharmas*) as both impermanent and devoid of self-nature, a basically insubstantial string of events mechanically linked by causal chains into an automatic merry-go-round. The enlightened attitude toward such *dharmas* is one which looks upon them without clinging or rejection, as a dream. This attitude involves being centered in the experience of one's deeper awareness as self-supporting and not dependent on mental phenomena. From such an experience of Being (which is also "non-being") it is possible to see beauty in everything without attachment or avoidance toward anything, for nothing is seen as either a support or a challenge to Being. In the ordinary samsaric, unenlightened position, however, we seek our fullness outside of ourselves (and in the past or future) and so become addicted to the peripheral workings of the mind, while undergoing an atrophy of, or alienation from, the central core of consciousness. Our mind, forgetting itself, creates forms that it may then grasp or produces thoughts as a preparation or rehearsal for a grasping action.

The practice of meditation, which involves the relinquishing of coping and grasping, shows how the contents of the mind arise in order to satisfy the subject's seeking of itself in an object. This is expressed in the myth of Narcissus who, according to the *Corpus Hermeticum*, fell into the waters of becoming in pursuit of his reflected image. This is no different in essence from the content of that other great myth about the origins of samsara where the basic cause is presented as a wish to eat the forbidden fruit of heaven and, as an immediate consequence, Adam's wish to "know" Eve. Images such as that of Narcissus falling in love with his image on the surface of the waters or that of the tempted couple in Genesis vividly express what Buddhism calls the dual mind—an expression equivalent to samsaric mind or ego. This duality, by which mind projects something of itself and experiences it as a reality to be incorporated ("eaten") or avoided, is the delusional root of ego, which sustains the passional (craving) and the defensive (aggression).

The ego's delusional notion is that the sense of being will arise or can be safeguarded by grasping (or eliminating) an object external to itself. (Attachments and aversions to objects in the external world may be understood as derivative to the attachment and aversion to mental states that they elicit in us.) In contrast with ego stands the egoless or central sector of our mind, which is at its core neither attached nor compulsively detached but non-attached (and non-detached). Instead of an overactive tension about survival, mating, and relating—that is, coping—we find towards the center of our being the gratuitous flight of a Pegasus (whose hoof striking Mount Parnassus in his flight gave rise to the Fountain of Castalia, the source of poetic inspiration). It is a state of not holding on to anything, no need to go anywhere, no owning anything, in which takes place a dissolution of the mental film as something in itself, as something independent of the creative act of the mind; a peaceful mental silence wherein is revealed intrinsic value.

Since Brentano, Western psychology has looked at mental phenomena in terms of the categories of cognition, emotion and conation, i.e., thinking, feeling, and willing. Mental events may be classified according to their locus in these three domains or in their interfaces, and they may also be looked upon as comprised of a cognitive, a feeling, and an active aspect. Any thought, for instance, though principally a cognitive act, arises in an affective context which influences its form and concatenation (as was shown by Freud in his study of free association). In the same manner it can be said to reflect our drives, our aversions, and our habits, both in the sense of automatisms of thinking and in the sense of conditioned preferences. Similarly, our actions and the will or impulse sustaining them are (except for totally reflex actions) influenced by an affective background (in content, style, or both) and by cognition (in content, strategy, or both). Our emotional life, in turn, is affected by our intellectual outlook or interpretation of reality and by the state of fulfillment (or frustration) of our impulses, intentions, or habits.

Through cognition we absorb the world (or—according to neurophysiology and Buddhism we form a [moving] picture of it). Through volition we act upon the world, changing it, and, in a sense, destroying or recreating it. Between these two poles, which are like the input and output of our central cybernetic system or the afferent and efferent pathways of our nervous system, lies that domain where the input is modulated and fed into the output. Thus the feeling domain lies at the center of this map of our being, as the heart between our two arms, or between brain and gut. Between our perceiving and our doing lies the sphere where we experience the impingement of our vision upon our predisposition to act.

Our vision, however, is a composite of sense impressions (constituting the input proper) and their cognitive elaboration. Cognition is sensation + thinking. Taking this into account we can now group mental events into four rather than three fields: sensing, thinking, feeling, willing.

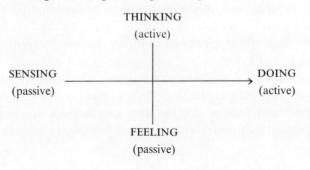

The arrow from left to right shows the flow of input-
output. Our elaboration of inputs and organization of behavior, however, are not ruled by a single principle but by
two: thinking and feeling. Both thinking and feeling are eval-
uative: they form judgments (intellectual or affective), according to different criteria of evaluation: true-untrue in the case
of thinking, pleasure-pain in that of feeling.

The four fields of thinking, sensing, feeling, and willing
may be likened to the four elements of antiquity: Air, Earth,
Water, and Fire. Thoughts are like the winds of communica-
tion, sensations are our earth, feelings our water, will our fire.
In the Buddhist Abhidharma psychology the four, together
with a fifth (consciousness), constitute the aggregates or heaps
(*skandhas*) into which are classified all the conditioned
dharmas,[4] or mental events.

To this geography of rabbit-land, which we may also call
the instrumental mind (because of its hierarchical subordina-
tion to a deeper and higher non-"mental" mind), we must add
territories that are ordinarily only evolutionary possibilities,
domains which lie beyond the boundary that delimits ego.
They are to the fourfold system something like a star to the
world of planets.

Some teaching systems point beyond our instrumental
mind to a Higher Self, who rides mind like a steed. Others,
further, spell out a polarity of two aspects in the higher realm,
analogous to that of thinking vs. feeling and yet not of the
same experiential substance as thought and emotion. These
two are sometimes designated as a "higher" (versus "lower")
mental and a "higher" (versus "lower") emotional plane, or,
better still, a higher intellectual and higher feeling "center" or
system. Still others speak of a triad, the third member of which
is a higher will: a volitional prompting from a different sphere
than conditioned responses and drives, which is experienced
and sometimes interpreted as divine or universal will. And if
thinking and feeling can be seen as yab-yum of yin-yang,
our higher will (manifesting only when "our," that is, our

ego's will has dissolved into a cosmic process) may be seen as offspring or "son" to this couple, completing a triad of non-conceptual thinking, non-emotional feeling, and non-passional willing. Other teaching systems, still, describe a four-fold system beyond the triad of true cognition, true emotion, true volition—as Gurdjieff vividly depicted (and without the helpful instrumentality of parentheses) at the end of *All and Everything* (Beelzebub's tales to his grandson): a passenger (a more analytical statement than "rider") to the body-soul-mind taxicab complex, which may be called the self in the strictest sense—for it is like a self within a self. Yet the word "self," because it connotes our ordinary experience of self fails to convey the open condition of the state beyond the *gunas*:[5] a condition which is like a field to their interplay, a no-entity entity that could well be referred to as a no-self self. The fourth domain has been called the Divine Body, it being the ground wherein may be experienced the secret identity of the mental, emotional (astral), and physical. In Vajrayāna, similarly, we find the conception of the Diamond Body in which Nirmanakāya, Sambhogakāya, and Dharmakāya are unified and of which they are partial aspects.

In the Mahayanist anatomy of mind, as we have seen, the highest consciousness (which could also count as a fourth, if the five sense consciousnesses are regarded as one), the universal consciousness, identified with the Tathāgatagarbha, is conceived as a store consciousness.

A suggestive word picture of the *ālaya* may be found in Borges' description of the Aleph:

> ...Really what I want to do is impossible, for any listing of an infinite series is doomed to be infinitesimal. In that single gigantic instant I saw millions of acts both delightful and awful; not one of them amazed me more than the fact that all of them occupied the same point in space, without overlapping or transparency. What my eyes beheld was simultaneous, but what I shall now write down will be successive, because language is successive. Nonetheless, I try to recollect what I can....

... The Aleph's diameter was probably little more than an inch, but all space was there, actual and undiminished. Each thing (a mirror's face, let us say) was infinite things, since I distinctly saw it from every angle of the universe. I saw the teeming sea: I saw daybreak and nightfall; I saw the multitudes of America; I saw a silvery cobweb in the center of a black pyramid; I saw a splintered labyrinth (it was London); I saw, closeup, unending eyes watching themselves in me as in a mirror; I saw all the mirrors on earth and none of them reflected me; I saw in a backyard of Soler Street the same tiles that thirty years before I had seen in the entrance of a house in Fray Bentos; I saw bunches of grapes, snow, tobacco, loads of metal, steam; I saw convex equatorial deserts and each one of their grains of sand; I saw a woman in Inverness whom I shall never forget; I saw her tangled hair, her tall figure, I saw the cancer in her breast; I saw a ring of baked mud in a sidewalk, where before there had been a tree; I saw a summerhouse in Adrogue and a copy of the first English translation of Pliny—Philemon Holland's—and all at the same time saw each letter on each page ... I saw in a closet in Alkmaar a terrestrial globe between two mirrors that multiplied it endlessly; I saw horses with flowing manes on a shore of the Caspian Sea at dawn; ... I saw a Persian astrolabe; I saw in the drawer of a writing table (and the handwriting made me tremble) unbelievable, obscene, detailed letters which Beatriz had written to Carlos Argentino ... I saw the rotted dust and bones that had once deliciously been Beatriz Viterbo; I saw the circulation of my own dark blood; I saw the coupling of love and the modification of death; I saw the Aleph from every point and angle, and in the Aleph I saw the earth, and in the earth the Aleph, and in the Aleph the earth; I saw my own face and my own bowels; I saw your face; and I felt dizzy and wept, for my eyes had seen that secret and conjectured object whose name is common to all man but which no man has looked upon—the unimaginable universe.[6]

The *ālaya* is the totality of experience, human and other than human, available to man as the reflection of all and everything upon the mirror of his (enlightened) mind; the projection of the macrocosm onto the microcosm, in virtue of which it has been said: "As above, so below." It is a conception which corresponds with the modern idea of the holographic nature of the universe as a consequence of which the whole is reflected in its parts. Hence in Buddhism *ālaya* is invoked as an explanation for the operation of karma as well as for the possibility of direct knowledge or *gnosis*. The idea of the *ālaya* may also be linked to that of God-in-us, the indwelling essence, consubstantial with God as a drop is with the ocean.

Even beyond the *ālaya*, Vajrayāna Buddhism speaks of a ninth consciousness, in contrast to which the eight preceding ones are samsaric: a consciousness in its primitive condition before it reflected, triflected and multiflected upon itself to generate the awareness of all and everything; a consciousness which is the root of all the manifoldness of consciousness interfused in the *ālaya*; a consciousness in its pure, original condition, in its egg or seed state, undivided and uncompounded; and this embryonic, primordial consciousness (which can be discriminated from the *ālaya* only by those who have reached the tenth stage of the Bodhisattva Path) which is to the octal system of consciousness like a central seed or star, is in the nature of awareness. Awareness in and of itself; awareness of nothing but awareness. Self-awaring. Awakedness, the "sacret" essence of the mirror. With such a formulation of the ultimate principle of mind, Vajrayāna, in its own style, tells us something that Islam expresses as "God is closer to you than your jugular vein." For awareness is the simplest and most irreducible fact of our awareness. Our trouble is that, as in the parable of the hen with the golden eggs, we seek the holy while desacralizing awareness. By devaluing what is closest to us we leave ourselves thirsting for value. The path of meditation is one in which we are weaned from support in outer reality until we may experience the ground of our experience of reality, and thus the ultimate experienceable reality, *anuttara*, the magician's invisible head within the hat.

Notes

1. Śākyamuni Buddha, *Udāna* (*Khuddaka-Nikāya, Sutta-Piṭaka*, Pāli Canon), as quoted in Lama Anagarika Govinda, *Foundations of Tibetan Mysticism* (New York: Weiser, 1969), pp. 58–59.

2. Padmasambhava, as quoted in *The Tibetan Book of the Great Liberation*, ed. W. Y. Evans-Wentz (London: Oxford University, 1968), p. 208.

3. Śākyamuni Buddha, *Prajñāpāramitā Sūtra*, as quoted in *The Perfection of Wisdom in Eight Thousand Lines and its Verse Summary*, trans. Edward Conze (Bolinas: Four Seasons Foundation, 1973), p. 57.

4. The Tibetan element attributions differ from those of Western esotericism, however: thinking–fire, feeling–earth, willing–air, sensing (form)–water, consciousness–ether.

5. The "three strands" (Skt. *sattva, rajas, tamas*) from which, according to Sāṃkhya philosophy, everything that exists is interwoven.

6. Jorge L. Borges, *The Aleph* (New York: Dutton, 1970), pp. 13–14.

Samsara:
A Psychological
View

Charles T. Tart

A belief common to almost all spiritual disciplines is that
man is ordinarily in a state of consciousness which can be
described by such words as illusion, dreaming, waking hyp-
nosis, ignorance, *māyā* (Indian), or *saṃsāra* (Buddhist). The
realization of this unsatisfactory nature of one's ordinary
consciousness is meant to serve as the impetus for either purifying it and/or attaining altered states of consciousness that

CHARLES T. TART has a Ph.D. in psychology from the University
of North Carolina. He has held teaching and research positions at
Stanford University and the University of Virginia School of Medi-
cine and is now a Professor of Psychology at the University of
California, Davis. His research activities are currently focused in
the areas of altered states of consciousness and transpersonal psy-
chology. His scientific publications include several books, *Altered
States of Consciousness, On Being Stoned: A Psychological Study of
Marijuana Intoxication, The Application of Learning Theory to
Extrasensory Perception, States of Consciousness,* and *Spiritual
Psychologies.*

are considered more valuable. I shall here look at the concept that our ordinary state of consciousness is samsara from the viewpoint of a Western psychologist, and share a partial understanding of this concept by showing that a good deal of what is said about samsara can be understood in some detail in Western psychological terms. This is not meant as a full understanding of the concept of samsara or related concepts, but simply as a way of expressing it which may be useful to others with some background in Western psychology.

Any understanding arises out of a conceptual system of some sort, so I will briefly mention, as context, my systems approach for understanding states of consciousness.[1] We start with the existence of some sort of basic awareness as a property of a human being, presumably a part of his nature given at birth. We also recognize the existence of psychological structures or systems, particular kinds of skills, attitudes, cognitions, etc. Within the bounds of a single lifetime, these psychological structures and systems presumably represent relatively permanent structures within the brain and nervous system, although one may deal with them on a purely psychological level. *Consciousness*, as we ordinarily know it in the West, then, is not pure awareness but rather awareness as it is embodied in the psychological structure of the mind or the brain. That is, our ordinary experience is neither of pure awareness nor of pure psychological structure, but of awareness embedded in and modified by the structure of the mind, and of the structure of the mind embedded in and modified by awareness. These two components, awareness and psychological structure, constitute an emergent whole, the over-all interacting, dynamic system that makes up our consciousness.

Orthodox Western psychologists see awareness as some sort of by-product of the brain. This reflects, primarily, their commitment to certain materialistic concepts rather than a real understanding of what awareness is. In most spiritual disciplines, awareness is considered to exist independently or to have the potential to exist independently of brain structure. It is well to recall also that this dichotomy between pure awareness and the structure of the mind and the brain is simply a conceptual tool, to be used where it is helpful, but not to be considered any sort of ultimate.

With this as background, let us now take a Western psychological look at how ordinary consciousness can be seen as a state of illusion, samsara. Figure 1 represents the psychological processes of a human being at six succeeding instants of time, labeled T_1 through T_6. The vertical axis represents stimuli from the external world received in the six succeeding instants of time, while the horizontal axis represents internal, psychological processes occurring through these six succeeding instants of time. The ovals represent the primary psychological contents in the focus of consciousness, what the subject is mainly aware of. The arrows represent information flow, with the labels along the arrows saying something about the nature of that information flow. The small circles with the A's in them represent internal psychological associations provoked by the external stimuli or by other internal associations.

Figure 1 is basically a schematic diagram of what happens in the mind in terms of the information coming in to the person and of the reaction to this information. Some of the effects in this diagram are deliberately exaggerated for illustrative purposes. The subject will look like a person who is psychotic in a rather paranoid way, but as we shall discuss later, his processes may not be all that different from those of our own ordinary consciousness.

What happens in terms of the external world is that a stranger walks up to our hypothetical person and says, HI, MY NAME IS BILL. For simplicity we shall assume that this is all of consequence that happens in the external world, even though in everyday life a message like that might be accompanied by many other messages expressed by gestures or bodily postures and modified by the setting in which it occurred, etc. All that

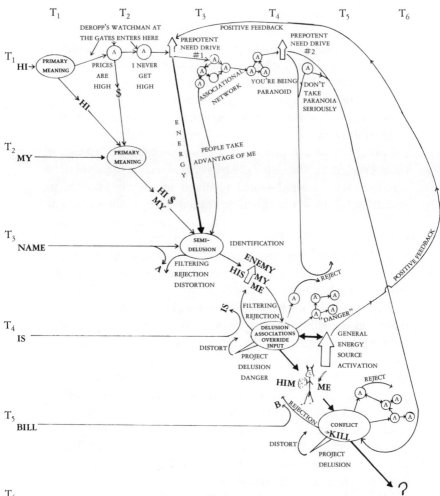

Figure 1

happens in our defined reality here is that the stranger says, HI, MY NAME IS BILL. This utterance occupies the first five sequential units of time.

At time T_1 the oval contains the label PRIMARY MEANING, indicating that the focus of conscious awareness is the word HI. Although we show this as a simple perception, it is not a *simple* act. The word HI, would be a meaningless pattern of sounds except for the fact that our person has already learned to understand the English language and thus perceives not only the sound qualities of the word HI, but also its agreed-upon meaning. This means that already we are dealing not only with awareness *per se*, but with relatively permanent psychological structures that automatically give conventional meaning to language.

Let us agree that the straightforward perception of the meaning of this word in its agreed-upon form is an instance of clear or relatively "enlightened" consciousness. Someone says HI to you and you understand that this is a greeting synonymous with words like "hello," "greetings," etc.

Now we might hypothesize that a relatively clear or enlightened state of mind in the period T_1 through T_5 would consist of the following. At each particular instant in time, the stimulus word being received is clearly perceived in the primary focus of consciousness with its agreed-upon meaning, and there is a sufficient continuity across these instants of time, i.e., information from the previous moment of consciousness is passed clearly on to the next, such that the meaning of the overall sequence of words is understood. That is, at time T_2, the word MY is not only perceived clearly, but the word HI has been passed on internally from T_1 as a memory, so one perceives that the sequence is HI, MY. . . . Similarly by time T_5, there is primary perception of the agreed-upon meaning of the word BILL, coupled with a clear memory of HI, MY NAME IS from the preceding four instants of time. This simple message of the speaker is thus perceived exactly for what it is.

A glance at Figure 1, however, does not show this simple transaction of primary stimulus information, but a much more complex process. My own psychological observations have convinced me that this much more complex process takes place all the time, and that the straightforward, relatively enlightened perception we have just talked about is a great rarity, especially for any prolonged period of time.

Let us now look at this diagram of samsara in detail. Again, we start with the primary meaning reception of the word HI at time T_1. At time T_2, however, there is not only a primary, undistorted reception of the word MY, but internally an association has taken place to the word HI. This association is that PRICES ARE HIGH. I have deliberately made an illogical association, based mainly on the sound of the word and involving some departure from the primary meaning of the word HI used as a greeting. In spite of our culture's veneration of logic, most of our psychological processes are not very logical.

The association PRICES ARE HIGH, is not obviously pathological or non-adaptive at this point. At a time when prices on so many commodities have risen greatly, it is a likely association to hearing the word HI, even though it does not strictly follow from the context of the actual stimulus situation. Where the "pathology" begins, where the mechanism of samsara begins operating, is in the fact that this association is not done in the full focus of consciousness but on the fringes or even outside of consciousness. The primary focus of consciousness at time T_2 is on the stimulus word MY coming in. The association PRICES ARE HIGH, operating on the fringes of consciousness, is shown as sending some informational content, or feeling about money in general, into the primary focus of consciousness at time T_2, but it is clearly secondary content.

If associational activities decayed or died out at this simple level, we would probably not be in a state of samsara. But psychological processes that operate outside the clear focus of consciousness tend to get out of hand, acting much the same way as implicit assumptions in logic: as long as an assumption is implicit, you are totally controlled by it, and it does not occur to you to question it.

Let us now further assume that the association PRICES ARE HIGH triggers off a further association during time T_2 because of the word HIGH. This is an association on the order of I NEVER GET HIGH. This second association then connects up at time T_3 with emotionally charged concerns of the person, represented by the arrow as PREPOTENT NEED/DRIVE #1. That is, given the particular personality and concerns of this person, he worries that he never gets HIGH. This is a constant, dynamically meaningful preoccupation with him which carries a lot of psychic energy. Now we begin to deal not just with simple information but with information that is emotionally *important*. For this particular example, this information is activating and has a negative, depressed quality to it. Thus the figure shows that at time T_3, when this prepotent need is activated, a kind of psychic energy flows into the main focus of consciousness. Also, the activation of this prepotent need/drive activates, by habit, a particular chain of associations centered around the idea that PEOPLE TAKE ADVANTAGE OF ME. This kind of associational content also begins to flow into the main focus of consciousness at time T_3.

Now let us look at time T_3 in more detail in terms of the primary focus of consciousness. According to how we have defined relatively enlightened functioning of this system of consciousness, the information HI, MY should be and is being delivered from the previous moment of consciousness at time T_2 to provide continuity. However, the relatively irrelevant association of high prices, represented by the dollar sign, is also being delivered *as if it were primary meaning*, coming from the preceding primary focus of consciousness, even though it is actually associational meaning which has slipped in. A general activation energy of negative tone is flowing in from the prepotent need that is active at this time as well as the associational content that PEOPLE TAKE ADVANTAGE OF ME. Because of the highly charged energy that goes with these associational contents, I have labeled the primary focus of consciousness at time T_3 as semi-delusional, because the primary focus of consciousness now begins to center around associational material while under the mistaken impression that it is centering around actual information coming in from the world. By identification with this associational material and the prepotent need activated, we begin to live in our associations, in a kind of (day) dream rather than in a clear perception of the world.

Psychologists are well aware of the phenomenon known as *perceptual defense,* of the selectivity of perception, of the fact that we more readily see what we want to see, tend to not see what we don't want to see, and/or distort what we do perceive into things that we would like to perceive. What we would "like to" perceive may often seem unpleasant, and yet it has secondary gains insofar as it is supportive of the ego structure.

To show distortions of perception, I have shown a partial misperception of the actual stimulus (the word NAME at time T_3) in that the A has been dropped out of NAME. I want to show that while much of the original stimulus gets through and provides materials (in this case the other letters) for later processing, some of it is dropped out. This process of filtering perceptions—rejecting some things, distorting others—is a major characteristic of samsara.

Having reached a state of semi-delusion, we now see that rather than passing the real information HI, MY NAME, what is being passed on is a distorted mixture of some of the actual information that came in, some of the associations, and the emotional energy that has come via the associations. Some fragments of later stimuli coming in are now being distorted to fit in with the beginnings of delusion brought about by the prepotent need and associational chains. Thus the s quality of the dollar sign ($) becomes more an s, and the HI turns into a HIS, and the MY then becomes opposed to the HIS in a classic kind of dichotomy. The letters M and E from NAME now stand in isolation, affected by the emotional charge of the dichotomy HIS and MY, so it becomes HIS and ME. Because of the intensity added by the flow of energy at time T_3, all the components of the stimuli may be arranged to spell the word ENEMY, further reinforcing the HIS-MY dichotomy.

Thus at time T_4 the primary focus of consciousness may be considered fully delusional in the sense that the internal, charged processes, the associational and emotional processes, distort perception so greatly that we may truly speak of the person as being out of contact with the world. We now not only have selective perception in the sense of filtering and rejection (shown here as the fourth stimulus word IS being totally rejected), but we begin to get the psychological process known as *projection*, where one's internal processes become so strong that they are projected onto the environment and wrongly perceived as actual perceptions. In this case the feelings about the conflict between "his" and "my" and about "enemies" and about "people taking advantage of me" now begin to be experienced as stimuli which are coming in from the environment rather than as internal associations. Other associational chains dealing with DANGER are being triggered by this process, including one, which we will discuss later, that keeps out competing associations which would not fit in with the delusional scheme.

I have also shown that by the time the person has reached the stage of the projection of his delusions with the negative content of ENEMY, and PEOPLE TAKE ADVANTAGE OF ME, he may now tap into his general energy sources and get an overall activation. It's not only that he has some specific need to think that people take advantage of him, he has now become so convinced that someone is actually taking advantage of him that he gets generally activated, generally uptight, in order to deal with this danger. This general uptightness not only pours a great deal of energy into the specific focus of consciousness, it also acts as a kind of positive feedback, reinforcing the prepotent need to blame others for not getting high that started the whole chain in the first place. That is, the fact that he now clearly feels himself getting uptight as this general energy flows into him acts as a justification for the need to worry about people taking advantage of him in the first place, further reinforcing the whole delusion.

Thus by the time we arrive at T_5, when the real world stimulus is simply the name BILL, the primary conscious awareness is a picture of a dangerous attacking warrior, with the dichotomy of him versus me very much to the fore. Moreover, this is not a simple, "cognitive" content, but one charged with energy, with emotion, as shown by the radiations around the figure, and represented symbolically by the spike on his shield and helmet. We can now have rejection and distortion of actual input to further enhance the delusional system. (This is shown as the B being rejected from BILL and the internal processes adding a K, so that our person in a very real sense *hears* this person say the word KILL.) This again is the projection of a delusion so that it is mistaken for actual sensory input.

The same associational chains triggered off in time T4 continue to be triggered off. (I have shown a pair of associational chains that were separate, linking up to represent a tendency for the delusion to consolidate itself.)

Now at this point we would certainly be tempted to say that this person is a paranoid psychotic, so out of touch with reality that he should be institutionalized (unless his particular culture values that sort of thing and makes him president instead). But this might not actually be true in social terms: there might be such strong, built-in inhibitions in the structure of his mind against *expressing* hostility, and/or such strong conditioning to "act nice," that the person would make some sort of socially appropriate response even though he was seething internally with fear, anger, and hatred.

The person is clearly at this point in a state that could well be called samsara or waking dream or an insane, cut-off state, though we have described it in terms of processes well known to Western psychology.

The fact that conditioned inhibitions may keep someone from acting in any way other than what is socially appropriate should remind us that the diagrammed process is not an exaggeration that has no application to you and me, but that some of our own processes may be just as distorted and intense. Again, while here things have been intensified to a paranoid, psychotic degree to make the points clearer, my own studies of psychological data, together with my own observations of myself have convinced me that this is the basic nature of much of our ordinary consciousness.

In some ways the presentation of samsara so far has been too simplified in assuming there is only one really prepotent need or drive that motivates us. Most of us have many such drives, so let us now add a second drive which will eventuate in a state of conflict and thus show further the nature of samsara. Suppose that after the activation of the prepotent need to blame others at time T_3, these associations themselves activate further associations to the effect YOU'RE BEING PARANOID, and that this activates a need not to be paranoid. This latter need might arise from a healthy understanding of oneself, or it might arise from the same kind of mechanical social conditioning that governs all the rest of the process. We do not need to consider the sources of this need at the moment, but may simply say that it also activates some further associations on the order of DON'T TAKE PARANOIA SERIOUSLY along with energy from the second prepotent need.

Figure 1 shows these associations (DON'T TAKE PARANOIA SERIOUSLY) trying to affect the primary content of consciousness in time T_4, but, because the person is already in a highly delusional state and his consciousness is completely filled with highly energetic paranoid associations, this conflicting associational message cannot influence his consciousness in any way. The particular route by which it tries to enter is blocked by the associations triggered off by the primary, delusional consciousness. There is no conscious conflict.

I have shown the same association DON'T TAKE PARANOIA SERIOUSLY continuing to be put out at time T_5 and actually gaining some awareness in consciousness by coming into the person's focus of consciousness by a different route. We now have a conflict situation: the person "knows" that this very

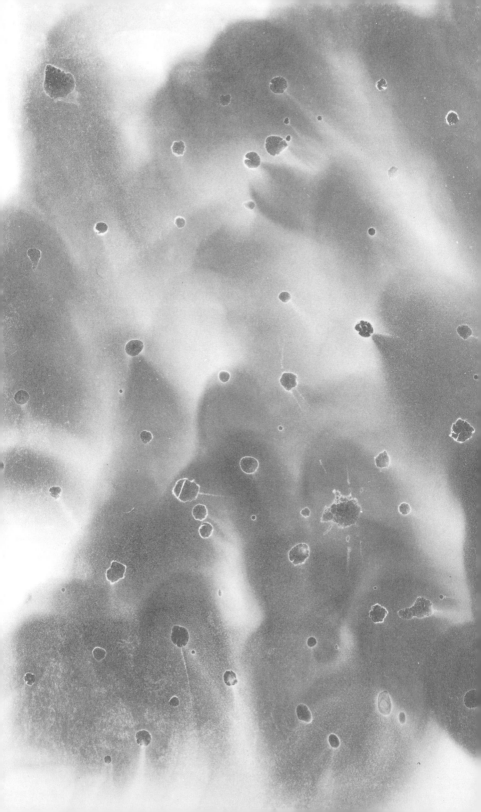

dangerous person may be threatening to kill him, and another part of him is telling him that he's being paranoid and shouldn't take this kind of paranoia seriously.

I have shown time T_6 as a question mark, as we don't know what the resolution of this conflict will be. If the bulk of energy and contents of consciousness are taken up by the paranoid delusion, the thought DON'T TAKE PARANOIA SERIOUSLY may simply be wiped out or repressed by virtue of not having enough energy to compete with the delusion.

What we have here, then, is a picture of samsara in six consecutive instants of time from a Western psychological point of view. The process, of course, does not stop with six instants of time, but goes on through a lifetime. If one were to expand this exposition into an individual's whole life, we could draw a sort of closed figure, showing a number of prepotent needs, which form the basis of the personality, continually acting on incoming stimuli in such a way as to produce recurrent patterns of experience. Thus we talk about a person as being *fixated*, as having a *personality*, as having a certain repeating life style which manifests in spite of changes in situations. That is, we say that in many ways a person is trapped in a certain kind of internal psychological structure that is maladaptive in dealing with the endless flux of the external world impinging on it. Samsara, then, is the automatic, mechanical operation of the structures, the machinery of the mind, a machinery which attracts and captures awareness instead of being guided by awareness.

Let me close by saying a few words about what "enlightenment" might be in terms of this framework, extrapolating from this account of samsara.

We have already briefly mentioned that if the person stayed with the primary meaning of what was actually happening, rather than having all his energy flow into associational networks and prepotent needs which then go on to distort incoming stimuli, he would have a sort of enlightenment—a clear, accurate contact with what was going on in the world. Considering that we start from samsara (because of the socialization processes), how do we begin to get out of this kind of samsara?

The first step in getting out of this kind of samsaric delusional system is the real recognition that it exists—not simply an *intellectual* acknowledgment of it, but enough observation of ourselves to realize that Figure 1 is not a diagram of some hypothetical, paranoid person roaming the streets, but a diagram of the nature of processes in our *own* minds. Only when this becomes a reality will we have the motivation to do something about it.

Secondly, a partial way out of it would be to begin to pay enough attention to our experience to start to distinguish what is primary stimulation coming in and what is associational material to it, and to study how the whole associational structure works. If we can keep the two distinct, we are less likely to get into actual projection and intense distortion of incoming stimuli. The diagram has these associational processes taking place outside the main focus of consciousness, taking place "in the dark," as it were. My personal observation, supported by some psychological literature, is that putting conscious attention on these samsaric processes robs them of a lot of their power: they can't function as well in the light of consciousness.

Another possible way out of samsara is the classical method of cultivation of *non-attachment*. The paranoid associations might still occur, conflict associations might still occur, but, in one sense, non-attachment means not giving energy to them, not *identifying* with them and allowing one's awareness to be caught in these kinds of structures. Insofar as one is successful in practicing this kind of non-attachment, one will be relatively free from the power of samsara.

There are cases of people who have achieved this kind of enlightenment through this sort of practice, for whom unfortunately it seems to fail when the person is thrown into totally new circumstances, as, say, if he leaves a country like India where a certain saintly style of living receives social support, and comes to the United States, where it doesn't. That is, non-attachment may leave the samsaric machinery, the psychological structures, intact, even while not giving them energy (although some of the structures may gradually decay if energy is kept out of them long enough). Thus if unusual circumstances come about such that non-attachment doesn't work, the samsaric structure which is still there can be activated and partially or fully take control.

Another possible route out of samsara is the Western style route of psychotherapy, which attempts to dismantle or restructure the structures constituting certain of these associative chains and prepotent needs so that they are not, as it were, lurking just behind the scenes ready to grab one's awareness and energy. This can be very valuable, but it can have the disadvantage that one trades one mechanical association-and-energy system for an "improved" model without really increasing awareness at all. Implicit in this statement is an aspect of my own theory on states of consciousness that we have only a limited amount of awareness, which also acts as a kind of energy. Ordinarily we let it be mechanically caught up in the workings of our structures, and so have little available for other use. Thus one may modify the structure and get a more pleasing structure, but not necessarily attain any more real consciousness.

Another alternative is represented by the label DEROPP'S WATCHMAN AT THE GATE ENTERS HERE, based on a teaching of De Ropp, a student of Gurdjieff, that if you practice a kind of self-observation or mindfulness continually, you will see these associational processes right at their beginning and, by giving them full awareness then, rob them of energy so that they simply don't proceed.[2] Thus if full mindfulness were practiced within the primary focus of consciousness, we would be unlikely to have these long associational chains building up and tapping energy sources. The watchman at the gates of your senses doesn't let potentially mischievous strangers into the city of your mind without carefully scrutinizing them. This would be another way of starving the machinery, the psychological structure, of the energy it needs to do its mischief. Such mindfulness could possibly obviate the need of cultivating great awareness of one's whole associative structure.

I suspect in the long run that a combination of techniques is best. Various kinds of mindfulness and non-attachment are probably the ultimate tools because of their generality, but there may be some psychological structures in the personality that have so much charge, so much energy, that specific psychotherapeutic techniques are required in order to dismantle them, otherwise they have too much ability to distort one's attempt at mindfulness whenever one gets into that content area.

Western psychology has collected a geat deal of data supporting the concept of samsara, in some ways studying it in far more detail than Eastern traditions have. Viewing such processes as samsaric may help remind us that it is not only those whom we label as psychotic or neurotic who suffer from "delusion." If this is samsara, then we are all caught in it.

Notes

1. Charles Tart, *States of Consciousness* (New York: Dutton, 1975).

2. Robert S. De Ropp, *The Master Game* (New York: Delacorte, 1968).

The Realm of Possibility

Arthur Sherman

"What is this work about?" "What do you do?" "What do
you hope to achieve?" These simple, direct questions, coming
from a sympathetic inquirer interested in Buddhism, ought to
be rewarded with simple and direct answers. They are not.
There *are* answers, but they are best offered with a bit of
preparation if they are to be clear and relevant. The difficulty
involves some expectations hidden in the questions themselves. Because of our expectations, we may be puzzled or
disappointed by the answers we receive, but also find ourselves hard-pressed to locate the source of the confusion.

ARTHUR SHERMAN, M.D., is a psychiatrist practicing and teaching in New York City and is a post-doctoral fellow at the Albert
Einstein College of Medicine. His background includes Gestalt,
encounter, and Fischer-Hoffman therapy as well as the psychologi-
cal/spiritual work of the SAT groups of Claudio Naranjo. He is a
graduate of the 1974 Human Development Program at the Tibetan
Nyingma Institute in Berkeley, California.

Three expectations in particular will affect our understanding of Buddhist practice—they involve its ground and foundation, its goals, and its method of getting there.

The ground—where are we?

EXPECTATION. We expect what we hear to be relevant to our condition as we *currently* experience it, to relate to where we are as it seems to us at the time.

We rarely question our ability to assess ourselves. We generally think we know ourselves, our lives, and the causes of our joys or sorrows quite well. When we hear of a new remedy, we check it against what we know about our own state of health. Often it seems the fit is poor, partial, or non-existent. "That doesn't really apply to me." "Interesting, but that's not where I'm at." But if we do not share the view of the human psyche and the human condition basic to Buddhism, all the rest cannot possibly be meaningful, for all the rest will be a remedy for an illness we do not think we have.

HOW DO WE VIEW OURSELVES? Those of us who are psychologically minded generally agree that much of what is wrong in our lives could be markedly improved if we straightened out our inner environment, our mental life. We understand that emotional conflict, dating largely from early childhood experiences, and perpetuated and reinforced in the present, creates anxieties and frustrations that constitute much of our daily experience and bar us from happiness. Western therapies have approached this problem with a variety of techniques founded upon varying theoretical formulations. At the risk of oversimplification I would say that almost all Western approaches share certain similarities in method and aim that may be more significant than their conceptual differences.

METHOD. Most of us understand the process of healing to involve a deepening of *contact* with the emotional turmoil itself. In the psychoanalytic tradition this is accomplished largely by verbal-associational techniques; in the human potential movement there is an emphasis on non-verbal and expressive methods (Gestalt, psychodrama, primal, bioenergetics, etc.). The subjective *intensity* of that contact is often the focus of heated controversy: "feeling" therapies demand ever more florid experiences to ensure psychological validity; other therapies counter with the argument that proper integration requires something slower and more intellectually focused than intense emotionality alone.

The issue of *specificity* also cuts across the verbal/non-verbal boundary. For instance, both psychoanalytic and primal therapies require detailed recollections of specific events in conjunction with accompanying emotionality—unidentified reactivity is not considered to be sufficiently healing.

These two methodological issues—contact and specificity —are also issues in the Buddhist scheme of things, and we shall return to them later on. But for the moment let us continue to construct a Western frame of reference for ourselves. We will need one—for it will soon become clearer that in Buddhism the "ground" or starting point includes within itself not only the suffering that brings a Western client to his therapist, but also the alleviation of that suffering with which the same client happily concludes his therapy. The end in the West is still part of the beginning in Buddhism, the solution still part of the problem. These odd statements may need some explanation.

AIM. Western therapeutic goals seem quite various and multiple if we look at the *statements* therapists make about goals. I would suggest another way of looking at the healing process which seems useful despite the risk of oversimplification. Let us start with clients and therapists who are subjectively content with the outcome of therapy and ask what seems to be the basis for their contentment. In other words, are there any parameters, or criteria, we can identify that those who have been helped by therapy would easily

recognize as valid for themselves? To what might they imme-
diately respond?—"Yes, I did accomplish that in therapy, and
I do consider that an essential ingredient of my contentment."
Let me suggest three such parameters.

1. *Increased flexibility.* Patterns of reactivity leading to
conflict and unhappiness will no longer be the only patterns
available. Being in a crowded room no longer produces automatic anxiety; being in an intimate relationship no longer
requires continual deference to the other; somehow it becomes permissible for *me* to take a vacation, for *me* to do
things for myself, etc. We feel a wider range of feelings, we
begin to engage in a wider range of activity, our thoughts
themselves broaden and open in content. Our increased flexibility leads to new possibilities and the realization of these
possibilities increases our flexibility. I think most people who
have benefited from therapy will quickly experience a sense of
familiarity with these changes.

2. *Increased positivity.* This refers simply to being in
ever happier, more pleasurable or more contented emotional
states, and being in them more of the time.

3. *Increased self-acceptance.* Here I am speaking of an
overall subtle but definite shift in our attitude towards ourselves as a whole. It is the feeling of somehow not being so bad
a person as we thought we were, that our conflicts are not
quite as reprehensible as they seemed. It is a change in point
of view about ourselves that is somewhat independent of
whether or not we are dramatically different than we were.
It is as if a parent discovered its foster child was really its
own—there is an attitudinal shift although nothing objective
has really happened.

Stated in this way, increased flexibility, positivity, and self-
acceptance are unquestionably worthy goals, difficult enough
to realize. For almost everyone, the possibility of making
them the basic climate of our lives is more than enough in

the way of goal. Nevertheless, we know that there is something more. Beyond flexibility, we sense something in the direction of the word, "freedom"; beyond positivity, something
approaching joy; beyond acceptance, love. These are our
hopes. For most of us, this approximates what we believe our
happiness might be. It would be hard to conceive of its being
anything radically different. Yet surprisingly, almost irritat-
ingly, a Buddhist would say that it is, it is different, it is
very different indeed.

At first we might not even wish to examine the possible
differences. There is something outrageous in considering
more. We are not that greedy. Our current vision is satisfying
enough. Yet gently, but insistently, our hypothetical Buddhist
would maintain that we do not know what freedom, joy, and
love really are.

We may be taken aback. We may think he is speaking of
some mystic ecstasy or else of conventional devotionalism.
But he maintains that he is basically a psychologist concerned
only with what is experientially verifiable. So what can he
possibly mean?

THE SITUATION. The Buddhist means to indicate that
from the standpoint of what he knows but we may not
know—from his standpoint of understanding—certain psychological entrapments and constraints present in our *original*
conflicted life remain *substantially untouched*. And he is saying they are untouched, whether we have worked upon ourselves or not; whether we are subjectively miserable or subjectively fully content. And these constraints, as long as they
remain present, will permanently obscure and prevent our
real potential for growth.

To someone who has gone down the road of Western
therapy without finding sustenance, this contention may not
seem unreasonable, although the "constraints and entrapments" are still unclear. But to someone who already has a

sense of achievement and satisfaction—whether as a result of therapy or not—all this must seem far-fetched. How might we still be trapped?

Again we have asked a forthright question. Now it seems that a process of consciousness-raising is under way. We are told that we are oppressed, and, as we may not have considered that seriously before, we puzzle about the nature of the oppression and ask for more information about it.

Somewhere in the course of participating in a consciousness-raising endeavor, everyone must deal with fear. We know immediately that this new process may upset an equilibrium that has become deeply engrained, however painful the oppression itself may be. What if we become convinced of this oppression, this entrapment? We anticipate that we will not be able to tolerate our current situation any longer, but may be fearful about or incapable of changing it. In short, we are afraid we will get stuck. And that anticipation and its accompanying anxiety quickly gears us for a kind of combat.

So as soon as we ask our very first question, "How am I oppressed?" we already have a problem of limited receptivity to what we may hear. The cause for concern may be very real, for from the Buddhist standpoint the oppressor touches upon all aspects of our being and all moments of our life. Budhism would tell you that your oppressor is your own mind.

This has a dramatic quality but does not clarify the nature of the coercion: How does the mind entrap? Here we encounter a difficulty unique to this particular kind of consciousness-raising: consciousness-raising about the mind—a sort of *consciousness* consciousness-raising.

Here we have no group in the external world to talk about, no oppressing majority whose actions we might coolly analyze. Our data is not out there, it is in here. We cannot know if statements about our mind's coerciveness have any real validity without looking into that selfsame mind and directly experiencing what is there.

We may imagine that we already know our minds. Indeed,

is not Western therapy a mind-knowing process itself? Most particularly in the case of the psychoanalytic "stream-of-consciousness" and the Gestalt "continuum of awareness" we have exercises that clearly intend towards knowing the mind. Furthermore the therapies of emotional catharsis, the physical therapies, and sensory awareness techniques all can be thought of as heightening awareness of our own functioning, and this, surely, is mind-knowing. If Buddhism is suggesting the necessity for a different level of mind-knowing in order to assess coercion, in what might the difference lie?

Earlier we spoke of Western methodology and goals as a function of the effort to increase contact, specificity, flexibility, positivity, and self-acceptance. Perhaps we can touch upon these things once more from a Buddhist perspective. My purpose is only to suggest the direction in which differences may lie rather than declaring what I believe them to be—to suggest the existence of possibilities. If we believe that there really *may* be something over the next hill, we have the necessary prerequisite for going over there and finding out. But if we think there is nothing there worthwhile, then the likelihood of our stumbling upon the other side accidentally is very slim. We will probably never get there at all, and we will surely never know what we have missed.

CONTACT.   What is awareness? Do we know when it is there? Do we know when it is not? Are there different kinds? A Buddhist practitioner might maintain that in our waking hours we are ordinarily never "aware" at all, even during our most intense emotional states. He would say that the state of being aware of ourselves while we engage in an activity is a specially significant state of consciousness and one that is quite different from "self-consciousness" in the ordinary sense of feeling awkward or socially anxious. He would also suggest that in certain situations when we suddenly "know" what needs to be done, we may be employing still another special state of awareness.

Even if we do work at times with such states of awareness, he might ask how long the awareness is maintained. Is a minute different from an hour, several hours, days, or a lifetime in terms of possible results? Often the awareness cultivated in an hour of therapy or a weekend workshop has a way of dissipating. When I do contact my experience, what am I contacting? Is it a feeling, or a derivative image of a feeling? Is it a person, or an automatic composite of old ideas, attitudes, and images about that person? Is it the present moment, or my idea of "now"? The Buddhist would hold that we are far from the raw data of unobstructed experience, but that such perception, free of distortion, is possible however difficult it may be to imagine.

In both Western and Eastern approaches healing and growth processes are crucially dependent upon contact with experience. But according to the Buddhist notion of what direct experience is, we are largely out of touch and thus proportionally limited in what our therapies can achieve.

SPECIFICITY. In the use of specific memories as working materials I think Western therapy is significantly ahead of Buddhist practices. Western therapy is not a waste of time, and such work with memories often has considerable value. Buddhist specificity, however, focuses on a more fundamental level—fundamental in the sense of dealing with questions like these: What is a thought? What is a feeling? Is it simple or composite? What is its origin, its evolution, its fate, its palpable substance, its ultimate meaning? What are the varieties of thought, feeling, sensation? How are the thoughts, feelings, and sensations we have at a given moment related to each other? Buddhist traditions of meditation provide for a detailed discursive analysis of such issues. Buddhism encourages intellectual integrity in pursuing these questions logically and rationally until we arrive at conclusions that are the ultimate end-points of logical analysis. It is a process which has the potential of radically up-ending our view of the world, our experience, the very nature of our "self." This intellectual effort is meant to establish the new frame of reference necessary for a journey of and into the mind.

But what constitutes the nature of knowing if we are setting out to know the mind? There is a knowing, it seems, that begins where everything we might once have thought of as knowing ends. It is as if we had planned a journey, consulting maps and guide books and considering the difficulties we might encounter on the way. But finally we must set off. The journey will not be a process of thinking about, but of ever more fully participating in, a process of learning how to learn that we may call meditation.

FLEXIBILITY. We recognize that much of our fear and frustration is ill-founded compulsive reactivity. We strive to make whatever inner change we can to provide ourselves with increased choice. Ultimately we may succeed in certain areas—we may no longer freeze inwardly in the presence of authority, or of the opposite sex. This increased freedom of response, which is so much a part of our sense of making progress, would be as valuable to our hypothetical Buddhist as it is to us. But he tells us we can go still further.

When it rains for days on end, a kind of gloom settles over us. When we are insulted in public, a spurt of anger or shame may possess us totally. What could be more natural? Yet we are not in control of this response. It happens quite automatically. When we are without friends, we assume we must feel lonely—indeed we do. We are compelled to, we have no choice, there is no freedom here. In the thousand minute-to-minute situations that comprise our daily lives we continually respond with reactivities over which we have no control. So constant and pervasive is this process—even in the "happiest" of us—that we take it as the norm and can scarcely imagine what real freedom might possibly mean.

Yet as beleaguered as we are in this picture of our lives, the driven reactivity in our mind itself is considerably worse. Shut your eyes for a few minutes and see if you can stop the flow of concepts, feelings, sensations, and images that stream continually through your consciousness. If you cannot stop them, perhaps you are in some sense possessed *by* them. Perhaps there is no freedom here at all.

POSITIVITY. What could be better than happiness? What could be better than feeling good, except feeling good more often? Are there pleasures, happinesses that are qualitatively deeper, more sustaining than others? A Buddhist would say that there are, but we know little of them—and he would suggest that we be less concerned even with them at this point. He would encourage us rather to question the "pursuit of happiness" itself.

What has been the relationship between joy and sorrow in our lives—do they depend upon each other in any way? Are there any elements in our pleasures that are already seeds of an unpleasantness to follow? Do we strive for unremitting pleasantness? Do we pay a price for this?

ACCEPTANCE. Surely genuine self-acceptance is one of our most cherished aspirations for it is a precondition for self-love which in turn precedes our love for others.

There is a crude way in which we may estimate our own progress along this path. It is based upon the observation that as love for others deepens in quality it becomes ever more selfless, ever more devoid of wanting or expecting anything in return. In the West, if we have developed some of this capacity, we will note this selfless generosity in our giving. Yet here, as elsewhere, the Buddhist standpoint is more radical. Extend this process of acceptance, love, and loving to its farther reaches until there is a quality of giving at all times and in all ways, completely devoid of any self-interest whatsoever. Total generosity, true compassion, and absence of self. Our

Buddhist means this to be taken quite literally—no sense of "I," of "mine," of "me," at all.

It is one of the paradoxes of self-acceptance that its realization tends to dissolve the ego. It is almost as if our ego stood in the way of this radical acceptance and love. But we can hardly conceive of what that state might be in which there would be no trace of "giving-to-get," and no presence of "myself." Yet radical and remote as it may be, our Buddhist would maintain that self-love falling short of this is only a shadow of its true potential.

These, then, are some of the possibilities, some of the directions in which we might move. If they are genuine possibilities, then the situation we thought we were in no longer holds. Our mind and its potential are other than they seemed. We may begin to get a wholly different sense of where we are, and consequently feel more limited, more entrapped. This new frame of reference is the "ground," the foundation of work, and itself requires extensive cultivation. If we begin to see our prison, we can begin to plan, in fact to understand the meaning of, escape. Without this vision, the gift of the jailor's key may seem quite pointless indeed.

The goal—to what can we aspire?

EXPECTATION. We expect a description of a goal that makes sense in terms of what we *already* understand.

Now it is clear why this expectation so easily undermines any goal one might proffer. Why should a man who believes he is free want to escape to anywhere?

In Buddhism the goal is enlightenment, realization, a total freedom whose incommensurable nature can never be fully translated into words. Here it suffices to re-emphasize that, insofar as we directly encounter the ever deeper and more subtle levels of our constraint, so also will we move towards liberation.

The path—how do we get there?

EXPECTATION. We expect to hear of a *logical* means of transit. Here again it becomes understandable that Buddhist technique will only be logical in terms of the problem it is trying to solve, and that one must have a solid grasp of that problem before any solution, however logical, can make sense.

If we set ourselves the task of investigating our own mind and its possibilities, how might we proceed? At first, we could simply *think* about the mind, try to understand as much as we can given what we know already and our ability to analyze it. We will encounter problems. It is hard to organize such an analysis and to conduct it past the inevitable blockades which themselves have a way of becoming fuzzy and undefined. A method of helping us through these difficulties is available in Buddhist tradition and is there for this purpose. It is called analytic meditation. It suggests various ways of asking questions and various subjects of inquiry. But while the questions are given by tradition, the answers are not. For implicit in this tradition is a radical empiricism which says we should take nothing on faith.

Paths of spiritual development need not be at all "religious" in any conventional sense, and Buddhism, among the many paths, is a form particularly concerned with independent experiential study of one's own mind.

This orientation to the "Path" may seem surprisingly free of the religiosity that we know is an aspect of world Buddhism. Buddhism is understood and practiced quite differently by various peoples in various cultural settings. But the existential orientation described here, as I understand it, includes its purest teaching—pure in the sense of making the fewest concessions to our ego-oriented expectations and desires concerning a "spiritual" path.

But when we try to answer some of the traditional questions of "analytic meditation," we find that we do not know how to begin to *experience* the operations of our mind. How might we undertake to do this? We must initially learn to set aside a part of the mind for use in looking at itself.

At first, the pressured, busy nature of our mental activity makes this a difficult task. There seems to be nothing left over that is not a thought about this, a feeling about that, a sensation of one sort, an image of another. We realize after a time that this pressured "busy-ness" takes up a territory in our mind that might in some way stand apart from the pressured stream, observing it. We may realize also that this process of standing apart involves an undoing of the "busy-ness," a kind of inner relaxation and letting-go that creates a breathing space for self-awareness. It is as if we were groping tensely in a dark room looking for a light, and stumbled now and then upon a cushion. Suppose that when we finally tire and sit down to take a breath, a switch hidden in the cushion is activated and a light goes on. In this process we begin to experience the difference between "groping" and "sitting down," and we begin to sense the consequences of the difference. In other words we are beginning to learn how to experience our mind, how to study ourselves, how to meditate.

This learning process requires skill and perseverance. It is like learning to play an instrument. At first there is didactic teaching: We are told something of the nature of the instrument and its possibilities and are given simple exercises. As we practice and encounter difficulties, we begin to understand the instrument—what will produce clear and vivid tone and what will not. Our questions about performing on it become more subtle, and we may find ourselves listening to old answers in a new way. We shuttle back and forth, questioning, practicing, experimenting, and questioning again, until gradually a proficiency develops that we can rely on, and the possibility of producing music finally begins. From time to time we may be given certain exercises to strengthen our technique, or our understanding of the tonal spectrum, or our sensitivity to sound. We may even find ourselves concerned with our physical well-being and life-style for we may see that these can hinder or help our performance. Ultimately we wish only to learn to play—to use all the possibilities of the instrument and of our talent, to play freely and spontaneously. This is the path of meditation.

This path, this learning process, need not be seen only as a long-range affair. Meditation has results that often come relatively quickly in terms of a more flexible, balanced alertness and calmness in meeting the vagaries of everyday life.

It is also important to emphasize that modern Western psychotherapy has its own areas of expertise, and that some psychological work of that nature can not only provide its own form of immediate benefit, but can prepare for, and assist in, the development of the more radical Eastern work.

The realm of possibility

The ground, the path, and the fruit. We have now touched upon all of these. Perhaps they seem other than we had expected—but we must be clear about our expectations. And it is well to recall that these words on the page which trigger images and thoughts are only that—words and thoughts and not experience. But they are also no *less* than that as well. These images are images of what might be: verified, they become the seed of what *can* be. . . .

The ground is entrapment. The path is knowing the mind. The fruit, is freedom.

Silence

Ralph Davis

Silence is at once a goal, a method, a state of awareness, a metaphor and a path.[1] While silence is many things at many times, it is always at least a metaphor, and like all metaphors it must eventually be laid down. The term "silence," like any other word or concept, helps map the geography of attention and is an indicator of the area of concern. But like the raft of which the Buddha speaks which, though useful to carry us across the river, must be abandoned upon reaching the other

RALPH DAVIS has a B.A. from Stanford University and a Ph.D. in philosophy from the University of Oregon. He prepared this article following his participation in the 1974 Human Development Training Program. He was then an Associate Professor of Philosophy at Albion College focusing on the non-analytic aspects of Eastern and Western thought. He has taught courses in interdisciplinary studies and Buddhism as well as courses in Epistemology, Aesthetics, and the Philosophy of Mysticism.

shore, so the notion or concept of silence can carry one only so far and then it, too, must be abandoned. In reaching towards higher levels of awareness one encounters many silences. There is an inner silence and an outer silence and a silence that transcends inner and outer, a silence of the breath and a silence of the body, a silence in the absence of words and a silence when the world is quiet, a silence where there is no sound and a silence that can be heard, and there is a silence that is a passage to emptiness, a silence of the mind in which there is no thought. There is a silence which is a response, a silence which is a truer witness than words. One is reminded of the passage from Lao Tzu: "He who knows does not speak; he who speaks does not know."[2] One is cautioned against attempting to make words carry a burden they will not bear. It is difficult not to see the double irony in speaking of silence. Part of the Tibetan Vajrayāna teaching is that truth is what is experienced, achieved by one who is enlightened. The rest of us can only point. Let me then point, make some gestures, and try to share some reflections on silence.

What is one doing when one seeks silence in meditation? From a practical standpoint, one's first thought is that quiet is needed in order to achieve silence. Silence, we expect, is not to be found in the midst of distracting sounds. It is at the same time very clear that the silence that is sought is not to be found simply by virtue of being situated in a quiet place.

Absolute physical soundlessness has been the object of acoustical engineers for some time. Their success has been only partial as is indicated by John Cage in his book, *Silence*:

... try as we may to make a silence, we cannot. For certain engineering purposes, it is desirable to have as silent a situation as possible. Such a room is called an anechoic chamber, its six walls made of special material, a room without echoes. I entered one at Harvard University several years ago and heard two sounds, one high and one low. When I described them to the engineer in charge, he informed me that the high one was my nervous system in operation, the low one my blood in circulation. Until I die there will be sounds.[3]

However, even though there is no such thing as a soundless environment, sounds may be present and yet not be heard. The sounds of one's physical organism may effectively be filtered out once a certain consistency of sound is achieved. Organized, patterned perceptual stimuli of any sort may easily become part of the background. The interest factor or the information-bearing capacity of perceptual stimuli is a function of its irregularity, of how much it stands out from its environment. One may, for example, sleep with the sounds of the street, the wind, one's own breathing, and so on, none of which is attended to, none of which is heard. But a footstep outside the door or a baby's cry—the out-of-the-ordinary— captures attention immediately.

One reaches a point very early in meditation where the quiet of one's surroundings becomes far less important than the quiet of one's mind. An outer quiet does not automatically bring about an inner quiet. However, often it is not until one ceases to be engaged by outside distractions that one comes to grips with the inner distractions. One then discovers an ever-changing scene of images, dialogue, chatter, noise, and so on. The English language lacks the words to describe adequately this activity, but terms such as "mental imagery" and "inner dialogue" may serve very well as long as we are generous in their application and see them as terms loosely defined and overlapping. "Mental imagery" primarily suggests non-verbal contents of the mind that appear or are called up in the mode of the senses, e.g., visual, auditory, olfactory, gustatory, tactile, and kinesthetic images, sensations, impressions, memories, and so on. "Inner dialogue" suggests the almost constant verbal activity of our consciousness, e.g., talking to ourselves, repeating conversations remembered from the past or imagined from the future, giving ourselves instructions, warnings, exhortations, commentaries, and so on.

Plato's notion that thinking is silent dialogue with oneself, although perhaps more misleading than helpful, has some truth to it. Most of our mental activity is, upon initial observation, primarily verbal in nature. This becomes especially clear when one first begins meditation practice. When one's concentration becomes diffused or attention wanders during meditation, one's mind is usually occupied with dialogue. When attention returns, one realizes that one has been holding conversations with oneself. There is a steady stream of words, conversations real or imagined about events or happenings, themselves real or imagined. These things are repeated, revised, or rehearsed over and over again until we weary of them or finally put them into a form that preserves our integrity or renders a situation acceptable to us. Our inner dialogue reassures us or destroys our confidence, tells us what we do or do not want to hear, makes distasteful things palatable or pleasant things unpleasant, and in general rearranges the world in our mind to conform to our image of it, whether this image be beautiful or ugly, positive or negative. The mind, it seems, cannot stand to be silent. It continually churns bits and pieces of dialogue over and over and glides from subject to subject with "mercurial curiosity." Even if this activity is accompanied by intense imagery, there is no slowing down of the inner dialogue which continues to work providing complimentary verbal commentary and evaluation.

This constant activity of mind, though perhaps surprising in its intensity, does not strike us as particularly problematic until one tries to suspend the dialogue. Then we realize its almost involuntary nature. As we try to relax and give our mind a rest from dialogue, words crazily reappear like the involuntary jerking back into consciousness when one begins to doze. And behind or below every dialogue, it seems, there waits another level of dialogue. If one's intention is to suspend inner verbalizing, the very intention not to verbalize is being verbalized. "Relax. Allow the inner dialogue to stop. No need for verbalizing. *No words.*" All words. More dialogue. Nor is this the end. Even if one merely resolves not to verbalize the instructions, one compulsively verbalizes the resolve. This process of verbalization and metaverbalization may in principle proceed layer upon layer indefinitely, each level remaining logically distinct from the one preceding it. Psychologically or subjectively, however, the steps soon blur and merge into one another. At this point silence seems further away than ever.

The notion that there are layers of verbalization seems at first to conform to experience. The procedure then is obvious—peel off the various layers until silence is bared. Methods start coming to mind to help peel away these layers. For example, I remember trying to accomplish this by attempting to divert the energies that usually went into maintenance of the inner dialogue to some other activity. Mantra has always had the effect of bringing me calm. If I concentrated on the mantra, perhaps the faculty engaged in inner dialogue would be deprived of energy, or at least its energies would be refocused upon the mantra. But as I concentrated on the mantra I was saying aloud, I realized that the inner dialogue was proceeding along in lively fashion, although it was altered somewhat to accommodate the mantra. Furthermore, there was now a steady stream of instructions going on within as to how to "become one with the mantra," to avoid verbalizing, to relax, and so on. At other times the inner dialogue was involved with conversations and observations having nothing to do with the mantra or the attempt to eliminate verbalization. It was most disconcerting to discover that the inner voice with its commentaries and instructions need not be affected at all by the mantra. I then hit upon the idea of saying the mantra with the inner voice, as well as aloud. With a little practice I eventually succeeded to the point where it seemed I could hear the mantra being chanted in harmony by two distinct voices, one inner and one outer. Much to my dismay, however, I found that in addition to the inner chanting there was still another

level of dialogue which was sometimes engaged in giving instructions, scolding, reminding, etc., and at other times was occupied with totally unrelated matters. As I tried with difficulty to harness this new voice, I reluctantly realized that this approach was futile. Not only did the various layers blur and become confused, but there tended to appear without my realizing it a very sharp and clear voice commenting on the difficulties and confusions of the other voices.

In addition to being futile, the approach was based upon a poor model. The idea that one can peel off layers of verbalization or dialogue as one peels off the skins of an onion is misleading. Unlike the skins of an onion which are finite in number and unlike the process of removing the skins which is finite in scope, there is no limit to the layers of inner dialogue. As was mentioned above, although the different layers blur very quickly psychologically, from a logical point of view they remain distinct and in principle unlimited. Thus my failure to penetrate to a final layer of dialogue beyond which is silence is most helpfully examined from a logical rather than a psychological perspective. The reason for one's inability to penetrate successfully the layers of dialogue is not that one lacks some skill or has not sufficiently developed a certain faculty but rather that the project itself is faulty. If one cannot, for example, accurately visualize in the mind's eye a complex and detailed painting, it is because one's skills in visualizing have not been sufficiently developed. But if one cannot visualize a square circle, the problem is not one of skill, but rather the impossibility of performing any task, the description of which is inconsistent or involves a contradiction. To embark upon such a project at all is to be blind to the fact that the goal is inconsistent with the described method of attaining it, or is itself contradictory.

I had proceeded as if the silence, or the natural mind which is manifested through silence, were something separate from myself. I would, as *subject*, upon successful completion of the process of removing the various layers of dialogue, encounter the *object* of my efforts. I was searching for, trying to locate, reach, or discover something. I did not realize that as long as there is someone who is doing the peeling and something which is being peeled, as long as there is someone who is working and something that is being worked upon, there will always be another something beyond the something one reached last. This is simply another way of saying that the category of the subject and its objects is unlimited. If there is something that is seen as being not-oneself or not-the-subject, it is always a something one can proceed beyond. The problem can be stated so that its inherent contradiction is obvious. "Attain silence by passing beyond the last member in the set 'the subject and its objects', a set which has no last member." Once it is realized that silence is not to be discovered behind the last of an infinite series, it can be seen that one cannot proceed through the subject-object relationship at all. Subject and object, *per se*, must be transcended. One cannot reach, find, attain, locate, or approach silence except by becoming it. One must be the silence.

The act of discriminating between subject and object is self-generating. The faculty of discrimination, the ego, is both the product and the process—the creation of its own activity. The faculty and the activity of discrimination must be dealt with simultaneously. St. John of the Cross alludes to this as he describes the flow of the soul towards spiritual repose.

> And the more the soul learns to abide in the spiritual, the more comes to a halt the operation of its faculties in particular acts, since the soul becomes more and more collected in one undivided and pure act. And thus the faculties cease to work, even as the feet cease to move and come to a halt where the journey is ended. For if the movement of going were forever to continue, one would never arrive; and if there were nothing but end-less means, it is hard to see where there could ever be a fruition of the end of the goal.[4]

The contexts in which the words "quiet" and "silence" usually appear echo this point. Although common usage exhibits no sharp distinctions between the two terms, careful reflection suggests a subtle difference in meaning. Quiet seems most appropriate to describe situations in which the subject-object relationship is operative, e.g., when everything becomes still, and sounds are no longer heard, one can observe the quiet. One may quiet oneself, one's pounding heart or restless mind. One may quiet a frightened child or a spirited horse, or one may quiet the sea by pouring oil upon the waters. Quiet may characterize the subject or the object. It is a term of discrimination.

Silence, on the other hand, conveys something different. Silence involves not so much observation or discrimination as it does participation. It applies most naturally when the subject-object relationship has dissolved. One does not strive for or observe silence so much as one becomes silent. Quiet may characterize what is or is not oneself, while silence pertains when the distinction between what is or is not oneself no longer exists. Silence is more inclusive and enveloping than quiet. Quiet describes the local and the limited which one may observe, while silence conveys the eternal and the limitless with which one may merge. Quiet is something brought about, the result of effort, or it is produced by not doing something, by not generating sound or activity. Silence is not produced nor is it the absence of sound or activity; it is what emerges in the absence of sound or activity. Quiet is imposed upon things, silence underlies them. Quiet is separateness, silence is wholeness.

The natural inclination is to ask *how* one can become the silence. But asking how involves the danger of seeing the situation as one in which there is something to be done and one need only learn the technique, i.e., *how* it is to be done. This, however, is a re-engagement of the subject-object relationship—the doer and that which is to be done. What one must "do" paradoxically is to "not-do." Silence is not something one does. Silence is what one is when one does not do.

The ways in which the subject-object relationship manifests itself are subtle and seemingly unlimited. So long as one sees the primary constituents of the situation as awareness and what one is aware *of*, the subject-object view is preserved. Silence is not an awareness *of* silence. It is not an awareness of anything, nor is it the awareness of nothing, for this would still be within the realm of subject and object. The silence of inner awareness is in fact quite the opposite of being aware *of*

something, for this awareness allows no discrimination whatsoever. Even the most simple and most germane of thoughts
such as "this is the silence," or, "this is the inner awareness,"
or "this is it," or simply, "silence," is sufficient to indicate
that subject-object discrimination is present. Our awareness
will not find silence in an inventory of its contents. Silence is
a way of being.

We are forever confusing the mind and its contents,
awareness with the objects of awareness. Many metaphors
have been used to designate awareness-without-an-object,
or contentless mind, e.g., natural mind, no-mind, emptiness,
oneness, the pure essence of mind, and so on. And though
their language may differ and their perspectives may vary,
spiritual masters from different times and places give us similar counsel.

"When no-mind is sought after by a mind," says Huang
Po, "that is making it a particular object of thought. There is
only the testimony of silence; it goes beyond thinking."[5]

In the Western tradition Meister Eckhart suggests that
silence is ". . . in the purest element of the soul, in the soul's
most exalted place, in the core, yes, in the essence of the soul.
The central silence is there, where no creature may enter, nor
any idea, and there the soul neither thinks nor acts, nor en-
tertains any idea, either of itself or of anything else."[6]

Awareness is boundless. Awareness has no limits. Any
limits of awareness that we experience are limits of our own
contrivance, self-imposed boundaries that must be transcended. The content of awareness by its very nature excludes
all that is not itself. Content is limitation. A given sound, for
example, excludes not only silence, but all that is not sound,
and all other sounds. However, it is seductively easy to view
awareness in a conventional way, not only as something that
is focused upon a given sound but as constituted by one's relationship to the sound. In this view, awareness itself is a category defined by its possible contents. This is tantamount to
determining the limits of awareness. If we encounter a point at

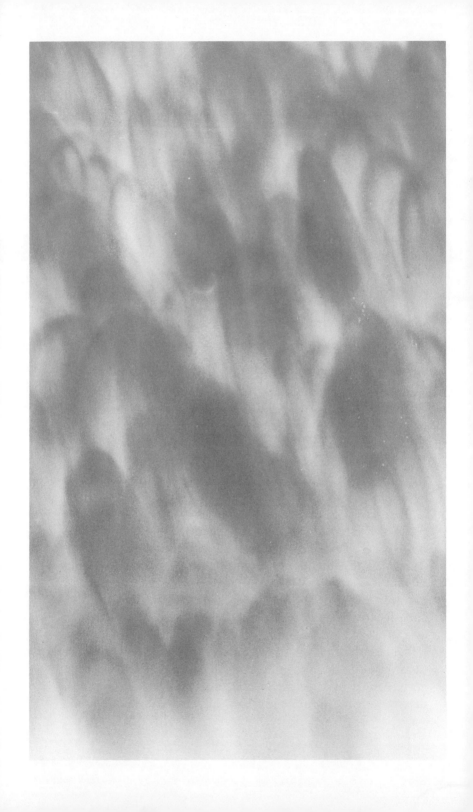

which our senses seem to let us down, or our mind boggles and
we must retreat, we then interpret it as having reached the
limits of our awareness. We experience it as an encounter
with content or subject matter that cannot be grasped. What
usually escapes out attention here is that awareness itself is
not bounded. Once we do distinguish awareness from its objects, then the limitations of any given object or content of
awareness do not in the slightest limit awareness. And if
we realize that awareness is not limited by the contents of
awareness, we need no longer experience the limitations of
content as the limitations of awareness.

As soon as one can let go of the identification of awareness
with its objects, or of the mind with its contents, boundaries
vanish on every side. Instead of boundaries there is a new
lightness and clarity. This is the boundless, this is emptiness,
that which contains everything but is itself not anything. This
is inner awareness and absolute reality. This is the pure essence of mind. A passage from *The Awakening of Faith* reads,

> What is meant by the Pure Essence of Mind? It is the
> ultimate purity and unity, the all embracing wholeness, the
> quintessence of Truth. Essence of Mind belongs to neither death
> nor rebirth, it is uncreated and eternal. The concepts of the
> conscious mind are being individualized and discriminated by
> false imaginations. If the mind could be kept free from dis-
> criminative thinking there would be no more arbitrary thoughts
> to give rise to appearances of form, existences and condi-
> tions. Therefore from the beginning, all concepts have been
> independent of individuation, of names and mental moods
> and conditions. They are in their essential nature of an equal
> sameness, neither variable nor breakable nor destructible. As
> they are of one suchness, of one purity, it is spoken of as
> Mind-essence.[7]

Here one has touched inner awareness, the pure essence of
mind. Silence is but one of the many gates through which one
may pass to become one with this awareness. Once one has
come to grips with one's own mind nature, one knows it,

understands it, experiences it directly. Everything that was one's awareness before remains so now except the limitations. Now one's mind nature is seen at the center of one's awareness and is experienced *as* one's awareness. As this inner awareness is developed, one finds that what was designated before as impossible was so designated arbitrarily. One passes beyond the boundaries of time and space, beyond logic.

Meister Eckhart has written that the inner awareness, that aristocratic agent of the soul ". . . is unconscious of yesterday or of the day before, and of tomorrow and the day after, for in eternity there is no yesterday nor any tomorrow, but only Now, as it was a thousand years ago and as it will be a thousand years hence, and is at this moment, and as it will be after death."[8] The very things that one had allowed to pose as limitations before, the contents of awareness, the mind's thoughts and concepts, the objects of perception, may later serve as vehicles by which to apprehend the boundless. The universe may be grasped in a grain of sand.

Anything at all may either bind one to the limited or free one in the limitless. Things have a side which they present when one views them as separate from oneself. They become the targets of one's actions, the subject of one's attention, the objects of one's awareness, the contents of one's mind. Under this aspect they form a prison that contains our awareness. The side that faces us is leaden and unyielding. A frontal attack upon these faces is futile. We constantly rebound. Our awareness becomes frustrated and involuted. But things also have another side, a backside, a side which faces on the boundless. On the other side of ordinary awareness, on the other side of sound, beyond activity, beyond movement and separateness is the essence of consciousness—unchanging, uncreated, and indestructible. Here there is no doer and no deed, no subject, no object, no acceptance, no rejection, only the pure cloudless sky where all is calm and clear.

There is always the danger of portraying too glibly the transition from one's ordinary state to the calm and clear of pure awareness. There seems to be some sleight-of-hand involved in climbing from one's normal plane to the rarefied atmosphere where the language is that of the mystic. This feeling is natural as long as one views the situation as one where there are obstacles to be overcome or a task to be performed. But this picture is wrong. Pure awareness, the natural mind, is not in some other place which can only be reached after a long journey. It is here. There is no prescribed length of time or painful apprenticeship required before one can be initiated. That which one seeks is present now. If this is the case, then what does one have to do?

The solution lies in the way one casts the problem. The question should not be about what one must do or what factors must be present in order to realize pure awareness. The question ought rather to be, why isn't one realizing it all the time? We are proceeding in the right direction if we look not for new techniques or new devices to employ, but rather, at whatever we are already doing that prevents us from realizing pure awareness. The term "natural mind" means just that. Upon taking inventory of ourselves, we find that anything other than the natural mind, the pure inner awareness, is something added—individual or cultural overlays which act as separating barriers which fragment us from ourselves. Subject and object, doer and actions, perceiver and perceived, are all distinctions foreign to the natural mind. These are walls dividing ourselves into different parts. We may scale wall after wall if we like, but the natural mind which is wall-less will continue to elude us. The walls must be dissolved. The barriers must disappear rather than be overcome. Once one understands this, a new picture emerges. One is no longer faced with insurmountable obstacles for there is nothing to surmount.

Separateness does not arise of its own accord. Yet one's usual state of affairs finds head separated from heart, mind from body, oneself from others. Maintaining this separateness, these fragments within oneself, requires energy. One is continually exhausted from the effort of sustaining barriers. One's energies are frozen. The mind is binding itself. What should be even, balanced, and smoothly flowing has been made concrete. One has fallen into the habit of rigidity. One must relax and let go of the tension required to maintain this rigidity. The barriers and imbalance are self-imposed. Frozen thoughts and concepts need to be thawed. Once we have surrendered the posture of separateness, and dethroned the ego's function of distinguishing what is and is not itself, then warmth and balance and wholeness return. Once the obstructions have been dissolved, light, beauty, inspiration—natural features of the natural mind—are unblocked and flow freely.

Certain pictures, certain metaphors are helpful in realizing inner awareness and regaining the natural mind. One must, of course, bear in mind that metaphors are only metaphors and that they will be seen as pale distortions in the light of direct experience. Silence is an especially helpful metaphor. "Each time you hear a sound and reach to its back side, there is silence." The metaphor is one of embracing the sound, rather than of subject hearing object.

"Become one with the mantra." Release the tension required to maintain the distinction between yourself as hearer and what is heard, between the chanter and what is chanted. When one becomes the sound, the sound disappears. Oneself, as something separate from the sound, disappears. Nothing has disappeared, of course, other than the distinction between oneself and the sound. Sound is separateness, silence is wholeness. Separateness is only present when one imposes it. Wholeness, one's natural state is always present. Underlying every sound is silence. Behind every sound which is a barrier, is "another sound" which is a gate. Sounds which are usually distracting can become supportive. Mantra, handled lightly, can suspend discrimination, separate sound, and allow us to reach sound's silent side. Within the natural mind nothing is fixed. There is nothing to work on. No sound. No image. No object. There is not even a mind upon which to work. There is no relationship to anything. One must relax, let go and stop expending one's energies on a fragment of oneself, the yearning, wandering, discriminating mind. Silence undercuts these expenditures.

The natural mind, inner awareness, which does not discriminate or separate is ego-less. Grammatically, there is no more first-person singular. A passage from the *Majjhima Nikāya* comes to mind: " 'I am' is a vain thought; 'I am not' is a vain thought; 'I shall be' is a vain thought; 'I shall not be' is a vain thought. Vain thoughts are a sickness, an ulcer, a thorn. But after overcoming all vain thoughts one is called a silent thinker. And the thinker, the Silent One, does no more arise, no more pass away, no more tremble, no more desire."[9]

Silence, ego-lessness, emptiness, and awareness cannot be separated. They cannot be attained individually. Space is a symbolic word and a helpful metaphor for this ego-less silence and emptiness. Awareness is a light in space. It is not a light against a dark backdrop of space, but the light of space itself, fresh and alive, a refined pure energy. Only "I" separates one from it.

Even the briefest realization of silence and seeing the ego function for what it is can affect us deeply. Once one's awareness has been cleansed, the emotions will find their proper channels. The memory is sharpened, for once the mind is cleared, what is stored is indelibly stored. Only after one has freed oneself, can one be of service to others. The non-fixated awareness allows one to understand and evaluate the human condition; it nurtures wisdom, and protects one from one's own obscure vision. Through the non-attachment of the natural mind the energies tied up in negative emotions can be transmuted. Beyond the negativity is thoughtless contemplation.

What before would have been separating, fragmenting occasions for attachment and limitation are now energy sources. No matter what happens in one's life, if awareness and meditation are maintained, what is truly valuable will be preserved.

Silence is a path to the natural mind, pure inner awareness. It is at once goal, method, state of awareness, and metaphor. It is principally as a metaphor that I have treated silence here. But there is a time to lay down the silence of metaphor and to take up the silence of meditation.

Notes

1. Many of the thoughts expressed in this article, and even some particular phrases have come from Tarthang Tulku, Rinpoche, of the Tibetan Nyingma Meditation Center, to whom I am deeply grateful for his teaching, kindness, and inspiration. He is, of course, not responsible for whatever liberties my writing may display.

2. Lao Tsu, as quoted in Aldous Huxley, *The Perennial Philosophy* (New York & London: Harper & Bros., 1945), p. 216.

3. John Cage, *Silence* (Cambridge, Mass.: MIT Press, 1961), p. 8.

4. St. John of the Cross, *The Dark Night of the Soul*, as quoted in *The Teachings of the Mystics*, ed. Walter Stace (New York: New American Library, 1960), p. 144.

5. Huang Po, as quoted in Huxley, *The Perennial Philosophy*, p. 73.

6. Meister Eckhart, *Sermon I*, as quoted in Stace, *The Teachings of the Mystics*, p. 144.

7. Aśvaghosha, *The Awakening of Faith*, as quoted in *The Buddhist Bible*, ed. Dwight Goddard (Boston: Beacon Press, 1960), pp. 362–63.

8. Meister Eckhart, as quoted in Stace, *The Teachings of the Mystics*, p. 153.

9. *The Majjhima Nikāya*, trans. Mahathera Nyanatiloka, as quoted in Lama Anagarika Govinda, *The Psychological Attitude of Early Buddhist Philosophy* (New York: Samuel Weiser, 1974), p. 114.

Meditation, Apperception, and Growth

Theodore M. Jasnos

The objects in our experience are seen as real, solid, and evidently present. We are aware of some particular object, thought, image, or feeling. That the world exists as we see it is almost undeniable. Everything belongs someplace. There is "my feeling," or "that person" whom I see "out there." We experience the world as an alternation of figures embedded in a ground. That is our "contact," our "reality."

One thought, perception, or image leads to the next. The process is self-perpetuating and ordinarily goes unexamined. Cognitive awareness normally illuminates the object of aware-

THEODORE M. JASNOS holds a Ph.D. in psychology from the University of Connecticut, Storrs. He has taught at Holy Cross College, received clinical training at the South Shore Mental Health Center, Quincy, Maine, and has attended the first and second Human Development Training Programs. At this writing, he was working as a therapist, serving as a post-doctoral intern at Elmcrest Psychiatric Institute, Portland, Connecticut.

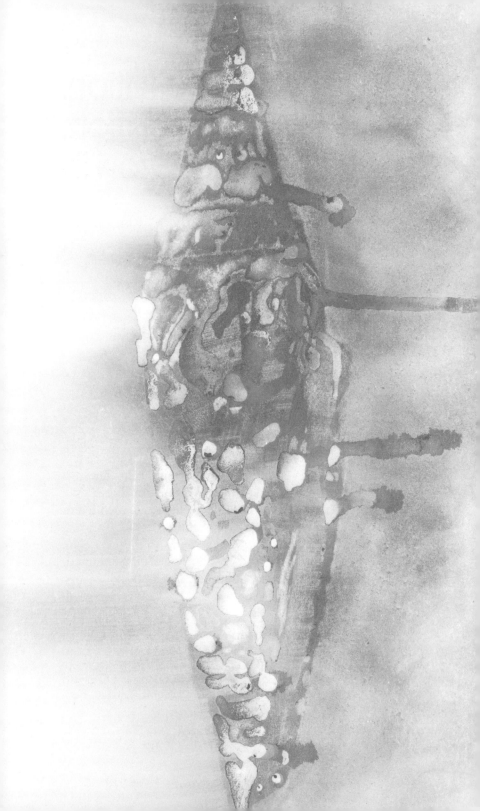

ness but not the intrinsic process by which consciousness of the object develops. A conflicted person, for example, may be aware of feeling miserable, but will then attribute his misery to his difficulty in making decisions, say, or to the complexity of the situation, or some such cause. Even if he reduces the conflict to its underlying assumptions, he will fail to recognize the intrinsic character of his predicament. From a Buddhist point of view, the basis of misery eludes every attempt at intellectual understanding, including speculations and inferences about unconscious processes, for the basis of misery does not lie in the contents of our minds, but in how our minds work.

Buddhist practice goes beyond intellectual understanding to a skillful utilization of awareness, which potentially illuminates one's predicament in the fullest sense. Meditation may be seen as a tool for fully appreciating and going beyond cognition. It is an experiential means of attaining knowledge of the intrinsic process of consciousness itself, that is, how consciousness of objects, feelings, images, and other mental events develops. Although full development and mastery of the practice discussed here may require years of practice and instruction, I have attempted to present its bare outlines and to show some ways in which meditation can provide a means by which self-perpetuating patterns of functioning can become fundamentally altered in the direction of growth and realization.

At this point an experiment in meditation is suggested. Although many techniques and practices are taught within the Buddhist tradition, what follows is a basic practice. You may sit on a mat in a traditional lotus posture, or you may sit in a straight-backed chair, so that the body is balanced and relaxed, yet poised in a position which allows free breathing from the diaphragm. Body and shoulders should not slouch forward. Your hands can rest on your knees or lap. At first you may find it less distracting to close your eyes. Later your eyes can remain open and loosely focused.

Let your body relax, and become aware of all tactile and

muscle sensations. Feel the pulse in your body. Without forcing relaxation on yourself, experience areas of tension in your body, and allow relaxation to happen naturally. Balance your posture, and let your breath relax and become smooth and calm. Let your mind relax. Allow all thoughts, sensations, feelings, and inner vibrations to flow smoothly, regardless of content or form. Without holding on to any experience, or comparing your experience with preconceptions, or trying to get "high," simply be alert and mindful.

Go with and into the stream of thought and emotion. Make friends with whatever is happening. Allow awareness to illuminate it fully. This includes the "I" who is having this experience or trying to avoid it. You may notice that you get lost in trailing thought sequences or fantasies. These diversions may be accompanied by a subtle fading of awareness and a loss of clarity. You may also get into a kind of heavy anesthetizing trance state. In either case, simply be aware of what is happening.

After about thirty minutes, you may become very relaxed and may also find clarity and awareness with a sense of greater space. Awareness may be bright and crisp, like the dawn high on a snowy mountain range. Mind may be as stable as the mountains themselves. Awareness may seemingly be everywhere—unobstructed and empty of discriminating thoughts. These similes describe one possible experience in meditation. In an experience approximating this description you may feel well-centered, steady, clear, and able to accept whatever arises in experience with equanimity. Closer inspection, however, might reveal that you are keeping yourself clear and centered. Your "will" may be working to keep you in that space which seems very pleasant.

Once your mind becomes calm you can go to more subtle levels. Continue to meditate allowing this "will" and your awareness to become one in the sense that there is no longer any difference between awareness and the "will" or center. The "will" or any other emerging center becomes the meditation. Continue this practice even with physical pain. Allow yourself to become that pain and whoever is withdrawing to avoid the pain. Any mental activity including desire, distraction, fear, and tendencies to repress feelings can be worked with in this way.

With this simple but subtle practice the dualistic process which separates you from the experience of an object can be transmuted. There may be a transmutation of the total space, including the ego or observing function. The ordinary process is replaced by another one which differs intrinsically from the first. The change, however, involves more than a mere replacement of one mental state by another similar state. There is a more pervasive change which goes beyond the cognitive and emotional functions. There is awareness, but not in the dualistic sense of an observer who stands in relation to something else. The "will" or "pain" in relation to the "I," for example, may no longer exist in its previous form. These mental events may be replaced by a simultaneous awareness as though one were seeing through all of the sense modalities. Through being in the center of the ongoing experience, awareness can become released from its narrow perspective. The sound of cars going by, colors and objects seen with the eyes open, and the feeling of sitting in a balanced posture may be perceived in an immediate and vivid way. The sound of cars may have no priority as a dominant figure over the bodily sensations. Both may be seen with clarity and without preference for one or the other. No effort to center oneself is required. Awareness is centerless. Tarthang Tulku describes this experience as follows:

> There is no need for any support, or knowledge, or any instructions, or anybody. There is no outside 'you' left. You become the center of the thought. But there is not really any center—the center becomes balance. There's no 'being', no 'object-subject relationships': none of these categories exist. Yet at the same time there is functionality, there is complete openness.[1]

Meditation sittings often seem to develop in two stages. First there is a preparatory stage in which the correct posture is established and the body, mind, and breath are allowed to come to rest. Effort becomes concentrated, clear, and centered. Later there may be a stage in which effort no longer serves as a center. Clarity may cease to be a goal. The technique, the meditator, and awareness are no longer "things" that can be distinguished.

Apperception and the development of consciousness

Buddhist tradition has elaborated and preserved detailed descriptive and theoretical systems which dissect what is phenomenologically apparent as reality. The Abhidharma, one of three major classifications in the Buddhist canon, is a voluminous attempt to systematize and elaborate what is taught in the Sūtras. The Abhidharma contains a model basic to Buddhist psychology, which views consciousness as a developmental process. Seventeen stages or thought moments are distinguished, beginning with an inactive state of mind, through primitive activity, perception, and finally abstract thinking. It is a developmental model in the sense that, for example, earlier stages in the thought process are considered to support later stages which occur successively. There is a progression from globality to differentiated form. The apparently solid world of form is viewed as being compounded of developmentally more primitive functions. This sequence is a process of "origination" which escapes recognition by the untrained mind.

Knowledge of the apperceptive process is gained through a very subtle practice that begins with the meditation described earlier. What follows is the bare outline of a set of guideposts developed within the Nyingma lineage over centuries of meditative experience and, for the most part, transmitted orally from generation to generation of practitioners. Although this system is not contained within the written works of the Abhidharma, it assumes the developmental model of the stages of perception. A knowledge of the Abhidharma may be helpful in understanding this system, but there is no direct correspondence between the two. In addition, this Nyingma system does not correspond to any way of describing reality that we have in the West. The function of these reference points is to guide one's practice and to make continuity and progress in meditation possible. The guideposts are not intended as an abstract system but as an inner set of vantage points for "recognizing" and "knowing" the experiential features of the origination process.

In what follows I have attempted to abstract from my own experience and from Tarthang Tulku's teaching, much of which was in the form of allusions and metaphors. Such a translation can never be direct. The entire statement is filtered through my own cognitive perspective. This discussion can only reflect my current understanding of a system usable at all levels of practice and understood differently at each. Also an intellectual grasp of this system should not be confused with actual experience. The abstract statement is only a map which bears little resemblance to the territory. It is difficult or impossible to learn these very subtle nuances of experience in the abstract. An accomplished teacher and a substantial commitment are invaluable in developing a practice which opens possibilities for and provides the basis for going inside the field of awareness and studying the apperceptive process.

The practice described earlier is continued into even more subtle levels of the thought process. Thoughts are entered and experienced from every angle in an unforced, open, non-evaluative way. Be there, go into the stream of thought, but also into what is not the stream. Go in between and within the thoughts. Go in front of and behind the thoughts or whatever units of experience emerge. This includes the sense of "I" and the self-image, both of which are forms of thought. With continued practice and instruction, the following levels of the apperceptive process can be distinguished.

KUN-GZHI: I will discuss first a quality that pervades my
whole conscious field. It is more than a matter of thoughts
imbedded in a medium. There is a sense that everything is
contained, or encompassed. There is a quality beyond and
within the thoughts, sounds, visions, and inner movements.
Inner movements and thoughts change, but the "behind"
quality" is there also, at times more inert, heavy, thick, inevitable—at other times more open, but not in the physical sense
that these terms convey. The term for this pervasive essence of
experience is *kun-gzhi*.

In talks given by Tarthang Tulku, *kun-gzhi* was discussed
as an experience-based term referring to a precognitive substratum or ground which contains all that is samsaric. It supports and opens to both the samsaric and nirvanic realms and
simultaneously embodies body, mind, and spirit. It is developmentally the substratum of imagery, dreaming, thought,
perception, and feeling. It functions in a pervasive way, supporting and infusing an ever-changing succession of forms.
Kun-gzhi is formless, with no beginning or end, an aspect of
a present reality which supports a many-layered universe of
human activity. The form of thought may change successively,
but the precognitive medium may be much the same. Out of
this substratum emerges differentiation. It is the store consciousness, holder of all residues from both the personal
and collective past, and is present throughout the cognizing
process.

It is possible to know *kun-gzhi*, but not in the sense that
we usually identify an object. The difficulty stems from the nature of the origination process. Any "experience" subject to
identification is not *kun-gzhi*. By the time the experience
evolves into the state where we recognize it as an "experience"
it is no longer *kun-gzhi*. For example, it is not "heaviness"
as such but what lies behind. The final "experience" is compounded of an extensive set of ongoing functions. *Kun-gzhi*
distinguishes only a primal level of functioning of the sub-

ject, the immediate experience of which is elusive to ordinary cognition.

Recognition is difficult also because of the fluid, ever-changing nature of substratum functioning. In depression, for example, metaphors such as thick, blind, or heavy might be appropriate for the quality of *kun-gzhi*. In certain meditation states metaphors such as "nothing happening . . . like opening eyes but no perception . . . vastness, speechlessness, or unknowingness" might be more appropriate. Light, purer forms of *kun-gzhi* are characteristic of samadhi states with qualities of blissful relaxation, clear concentrated attention, or emptiness.

Emotions such as anger, envy, and hate have strong *kun-gzhi* characteristics. As emotion intensifies, consciousness dissolves into *kun-gzhi* and other functions of the apperceptive process. Conscious discernment and mindfulness become difficult and one is unknowingly immersed.

Recognizing *kun-gzhi* and meditating in such a way that *kun-gzhi* becomes lighter is vitally important. Total realization is being completely out of *kun-gzhi* and hence the entire samsaric round of functioning. Nirvana is from substratum up original and unformed. Yet, the nirvanic perspective does not exist apart from samsara. One cannot exist without the other. *Kun-gzhi* is as much the ground of enlightenment as of stupidity and delusion. Thus *kun-gzhi* cannot be considered a negative process. Going beyond or transmuting *kun-gzhi* requires both recognition and the finest practice. Openness, clarity, freshness, relaxation, naturalness, and awareness are qualities of experience indicating the proper direction. Grasping, fixation, stupor, dullness, and anesthetizing trance states are important to recognize, but a hindrance when pursued as objectives.

KUN-GZHI RNAM-SHES: Continue looking in between thoughts, in those spaces that we usually overlook or forget about when one thought sequence shifts to another. As the space expands, images may start to flow as if to fill a vacuum. Memories from childhood may emerge. Staying with the flow of images, feelings, thoughts, the non-flow in between, and the intrinsic qualities within these units, mind becomes balanced. A "qualified observer" remains who is untroubled by who he is, where he is, or what there is to observe. This "observer" is awareness, accepting and embodying its own nature, with no place to go, and no need to hold on. In this field there is a very fine activity, a mirror-like quality. With the eyes open, objects in the field of vision take on this quality. It is purity and clarity. This quality is there an instant before the sound of a bell, the first part of the rub or squeak before you think. The not-quite-yet just prior to moving as you get out of a chair. This quality is initially easier to recognize at the first instant of thought or action but is also present during abstract thought. It can be seductively engaging and intoxicating. This very real quality of lived experience available with each thought in the observer who knows how to look is *kun-gzhi rnam-shes*.

My understanding of *kun-gzhi rnam-shes*, based on lectures and experience, is that the term refers to the initial occurrence of activity and movement in the field, the characteristic that is already manifesting out of *kun-gzhi*. It defines the initial activity in a nearly instantaneous process, culminating in grasping, attachment, and abstract thought but is not yet any of these. The basis for a subject-object distinction is only beginning. With this evasive glimmer of activity, apperception begins. Tarthang Tulku used metaphors such as a "mirror-like vision of a man twenty miles away . . . something looking, or moving far in the distance . . . perception is there, not here." There is a "flavor of purity and clarity, but the light is pale, not bright, like on a cloudy day . . . an unknowing perception but not yet perception, not yet thought." "Like a monkey, it is excited and never rests." It flavors thought but is usually ignored during thought. It is given as subject and not object. You cannot look back on it, or it is lost, but it is possible to have knowledge of *kun-gzhi rnam-shes* as an inherent characteristic of an emergent reality.

YID: As *kun-gzhi rnam-shes* becomes more activated, clarity increases, becoming perception but not yet discrimination and grasping. This function is *yid*. With characteristic humor Tarthang Tulku commented that symbolically *kungzhi* and *kun-gzhi rnam-shes* could be seen as female and male. The foetus, formed a few weeks after coitus, could represent *yid*. In nine months comes *nyon-yid*, which is the birth of "grasping mind."

My own experience of *yid* is of a rapid arrest emerging out of the vast pervasiveness of *kun-gzhi*, through an initial activity, (*kun-gzhi rnam-shes*) into a rubbing, twisting, or squeaking, to a totally sharp, located perception. My understanding is that *yid* refers to the point of articulation, the rubbing, twisting, or squeaking of the perception coming into being. *Yid* is like a sliding motion which is crucial to presenting the world as it is coming to be presented. *Kun-gzhi* is the holder of residues, *yid* is the mid-point at which these residues are actualized and coming into experience. The sensing of sight, sound, touch, smell, and taste is made into the perception by the *yid* in an action that arises out of a faint glimmer and "hits to" categorical perception.

NYON-YID: *Nyon-yid* refers to a function which triggers and conveys emotion and self-image. According to Tarthang Tulku, one half of the way through the *nyon-yid* is the beginning of the *kāmadhātu* or desire realm. One is then completely immersed in samsaric mind. Just previous to this stage, there was perception but no preference. At the *nyon-yid* level the positive or negative bias that infuses the grasping mind is established. The movement toward or away from the object of perception is inescapable at this point. One does not know which desire is coming next. With conflicting emotions the situation becomes more complex. Tarthang Tulku once described depression, for example, as a highly compounded state involving conflicting emotions. There is "a strong will pushing *nyon-yid* into *kun-gzhi*, like jamming it into a corner." In this condition one does not want to see the world. Higher level abstractions and beliefs were viewed as feeding into the process, further compounding basic conflicts and maintaining the depression. This is one example of how emotional states may be understood by someone adept at using this system.

The action of *nyon-yid* also provides what Tarthang Tulku described as the "current" which conveys and triggers both the self-image and the observing function generally referred to as ego. The action is subtle, quick, and not conceptual. Self-image at the *nyon-yid* level is like an experience of immediate touching, the barest recognition of a definite, discriminable characteristic directly referred to a center and experienced as belonging to me. Tarthang Tulku commented that if the *nyon-yid* did not function we would "have no place." This experience of belonging someplace is available all the time.

SELF-IMAGE AND EGO: At the *nyon-yid* level there is at first only clear separation and a sense of position. This now becomes further compounded, and from here on we are in territory more familiar to Western psychology. Tarthang Tulku's use of the term self-image included not only what a person might consciously identify in reference to himself but also unconscious and preconscious processes of the sort included in the Jungian concept of the shadow, the inferior side that "belongs here" but which we are unwilling to see or express. This establishes a set of relatively autonomous functions expressed via projection as "belonging there." Meditation involves a process of becoming fully conscious of, assimilating, and going beyond the fragmented aspects of personality which we have compounded in a highly complex self-image.

An article on self-image by Tarthang Tulku provided a discussion of the advanced stages of this compounding of self-image, beginning with an "I" which experiences, feels, and sees things in an alive and immediate way.[2] This "I" becomes imbued with thoughts such as "I am inadequate ... lonely ... or guilty," and the person begins to act as though he were someone else. He acts on the basis of self-generated images and deductions which continue as long as the process is fed. For example, "I am guilty" can feed into "I don't deserve to succeed" which in turn can feed into "I can't do it" which can conflict with "I've got to do it." The process can continue interminably and make responsive and spontaneous action impossible.

Tarthang Tulku stated in a lecture that when the self-image starts, then ego is already there. The ego is alive, definitely there, a more "separate entity like a wall or an object." The term ego was used to imply an element of proudness, an absolute conviction that "it is me!" The more rigid and proud the ego, the greater the awareness of its own fragility. There is a fear of loss of identity or loss of objects and persons whom we unconsciously include as a part of our identity. Such loss would, in fantasy, expose us to chaos, unacceptable feelings of discomfort, and loss of control. Defense becomes a primary ego function. Denial, repression, rationalization, escape, compromise, camouflage, rigid character traits, and other mechanisms all function further to complicate the samsaric situation.

In practice, the experience of recognizing each level of apperception distinguished in this system is different. With every change in locus of observation there is a different view. From one point of view it is possible to be aware of form emerging out of *kun-gzhi*, like an image coming out of the sky. This seems to necessitate a stepping aside and creation of duality in experience. This may seem to happen the moment we recognize any aspect of the apperceptive process. A recognition of *kun-gzhi, yid*, or self-concept, for example, seems to imply relativity. The quality of actual awareness, however, changes during meditation in which such recognition occurs. There is an increase in clarity, precision, and presence of

mind. In fully becoming the observer, the apperceptive process is transformed at all levels, *kun-gzhi* through ego. The
observation process and the effort disappear. Lama Mi-
pham's statement, "Meditation is the constant spontaneity
... of coincident Emptiness and relativity,"[3] seems to convey the nature of this practice. A practice directed toward
knowing only the relativity of this system without the spontaneity that is neither openness nor form would be self
limiting.

The context of growth: samsara and nirvana

From a Buddhist perspective, the potential for growth is
not bounded by or limited to the samsaric condition. The limit
of human potential is not confined to cognitively specified
goals such as adjustment to society, good interpersonal relations, adequate ego functioning, and a pleasant character. In
addition to such goals, the Buddhist context of growth includes insight into levels of the apperceptive process that
have not been explored systematically in Western introspective efforts, and it implies the immanent possibility of full
enlightenment.

For this reason it is necessary to discuss the relationship
between samsara and nirvana.

> In Buddhism, there is only a very subtle distinction between
> samsara and nirvana. It means there aren't really any differences
> between the world and heaven. It's only a matter of realizing or
> not realizing it. And whether we realize it or not, or reach that
> state or not, depends on very little, because there's really no
> difference between the two. It's even difficult to know which side
> of the coin is realization and which is not realization—they're
> both the same coin. If one side of the coin is not there, the
> other side can't be there. If the front side of my hand doesn't
> exist, the back side cannot exist. Similarly, if this consciousness
> or this mind or this thought does not exist, then my meditation
> cannot survive.

That meditation, that nirvana is so close—there's no time and distance. We have words naming it, but it's only a word: *nowness.* When there is no time or distance, we call it nowness, this very moment, the presence of your mind, the presence of your thought.[4]

The statement that there is "really no difference between samsara and nirvana" is traditional. If there is no difference, we might ask, why is it necessary to talk about changing, or growth, or meditation, all of which seems to suggest that there is someplace different to go. This paradox is perhaps impossible to resolve rationally. One way of understanding it is to assume that it exists only at a logical level and arises out of an attempt to describe reality from two perspectives. Of these two, only the samsaric perspective lends itself to cognitive description and to a preoccupation with differences. Experiencing oneself as being "this way" or "here" relative to the possibility of being "somehow else" or "in another place" is one prominent characteristic of the samsaric perspective. From a perspective which creates these dualities, there seems to be an obvious difference between samsara and nirvana, and it seems to be necessary to talk about meditation and growth. From the perspective of realization where there is full presence of mind, the cognitive distinction between samsara and nirvana may not appear. The nirvanic side and the samsaric side are seen to be "simultaneously coexistent." We may then say that there is no difference between samsara and nirvana or that nirvana is simply "being" with no place to go.

A number of statements made by Tarthang Tulku and appearing in texts suggest that from the Buddhist perspective of enlightenment, that is, from the viewpoint of a realized person, change involving reorganization of defenses, personal cosmology, character, or self-image is of little significance. We may rearrange our lives somewhat and feel better. We can move away from our parents, get a divorce, work on a new self-image, or, in meditation, contemplate the meaning of a limitless succession of images, symbols, and dreams. Such

Entrance to the Nyingma Institute, site of the Human Development Training Programs.

change and contemplation may be seen as an integral part of a growth process from the perspective of a person involved in that process. From the perspective of realization, however, such changes are incidental. A preoccupation with rearranging the objects of our existence may only perpetuate our involvement in samsara. Although life may improve to our temporary satisfaction, samsaric mind by its nature perpetuates its own activity of which dissatisfaction is an integral part.

In samsaric functioning the world becomes organized into meaningful units. What "belongs to me" is seen in relation to what "belongs there." This appearance of solidity fills temporarily a deep longing for fusion, closeness, and safety, but also feeds the fear of its opposite, loss, non-existence, and absence of center.

At the *nyon-yid* level, we experience a movement toward, away from, or become indifferent to objects in our experience. Pleasant experiences are those which we would like to have again. Unpleasant experiences are those which we would like to be rid of. In indifference neither of these desires is dominant. Our experience is more or less imbued with these affective orientations, and action is based on emotional preference. There is an alternation of pleasure and displeasure, good and evil, love and hate, which lends itself to description in terms of cause and effect. The horizon always has a beyond, the road is always long, every feeling has its opposite, and dissatisfaction is immanent.

From a samsaric perspective, life may be viewed as a cause-effect, action-reaction process in which a formed goal is pursued. Attainment of the goal tends to be the best outcome under the best conditions. Mind focused on control and possession of material objects becomes thick, solid, and heavy like matter. If mind is occupied with itself and the control of emotions, thoughts, and how we impress others, control can be achieved, but at the expense of spontaneity. Mind acting on itself neutralizes vitality and becomes impotent. Action becomes unresponsive to the situation and bound by inner conflict. Likewise, mind reaching for the sublime, eternal bliss, universal consciousness, may attain that goal and then vibrate with joy—temporarily. Aspiring to heaven, the highest samadhi, or any state which satisfies one's passion can mean success, and a long stay, but then also eventual dissatisfaction.

In meditation, for example, we may try hard to prolong what we experience as a very "high" state, even to the point of straining to cross our eyes or to maintain a very painful position. Where there is tight "fixing," forced concentration, and attachment of this nature, there is a buildup of tension, or an increasing stagnation which eventually results in an explosion. We may undergo temporary disorganization, diffuse autonomic response, depression, or, on the other hand, creative restructuring and insight. This phenomenon is particularly notable following intense meditations or exercises where there is a strong effort to "go all the way," forcing a particular mental state or pitting oneself against very intense pain. Experientially the "rebound" may seem either impressive or discouraging, depending on what happens and one's perspective or point of view. From the viewpoint of enlightenment, however, limited goals have been attained or lost. In either case, we fall short of full realization. The round of samsaric functioning is unbroken.

Another characteristic of samsaric functioning is that one thought leads to another automatically. There is no sense of what happens from one thought to another. First we are here, now we are in another place, forgetting where we just were and how the sequence just happened. Samsaric mind ignores the spaces in between the units of thought and experience. The continuity of awareness is lost in the midst of a fluctuating quest for bliss and flight from suffering. There are brief but significant losses of consciousness which occur outside of the focus of ordinary attention. It is partially because of the lapses in consciousness that samsaric functioning is cyclical and repetitive in nature.

These repetitive cycles can be seen as units of action and experience which operate on the basis of preference and revolve around some object or goal defined by our cognitive viewpoint. Alternatively, we may remain indifferent, passive, and subject to outside influence. There are an infinite number of goals to set and choices to make, and an infinite number of ways of viewing oneself and the world. We could describe as many action-reaction patterns as we would care to discern. Samsara could be viewed as a set of action-reaction cycles operating at potentially an infinite number of levels.

Implications for growth

As with psychotherapy, the outcome of even an extended meditation practice is uncertain. The effectiveness of meditation is influenced by a great number of factors, including mindfulness, alertness, amount of experience, knowledge, and guidance from an accomplished teacher. There may be little growth or change, or merely a resynthesis of the previous reality or character style in all of its essential aspects. This can happen even with high motivation for growth and a commitment to meditation as a means. One might change, for example, from a compulsive accountant to a compulsive meditator, who itemizes his "mystical experiences" with little change in the way he "does business." He may continue approaching meditation in a deliberate, rigid, and even dogmatic way. There is little relief or growth in this kind of change and some danger of self-deception.

Alternatively, meditation can create conditions for significant growth. Experiences such as those described previously may be brief, momentary, and even difficult to recognize. The first reaction is to think about what happened. By the time you think about it, cognitive development has formed "an experience" which has the quality of ordinary consciousness. All of a sudden you and the "experience" belong someplace. A fundamental duality is created. But even a temporary transformation in the constant flow of ideation during meditation may play a significant role in the growth process as may openness, relaxation, and spontaneous mindfulness of a meditative attitude in everyday life. In this section I attempt to describe some of the conditions created in meditation and to discuss some ways in which these conditions may foster change in the direction of more complete realization.

The meditative process seems to involve a very complete assimilation—contacting and becoming more fully aware of objects, images, and feelings as they evolve. There is a continuous unfolding of what is not fully conscious but is nevertheless inherent in the meditator's self-image, character, or style of functioning at the moment. For the period of practice, awareness illuminates the self-image, ego, and various subtle aspects of these formed objects of experience. The present moment becomes transformed in a way that might be conceptualized as a reduction of distance between the aware observing function and its object until contact is made. At this point the boundaries of the observing function expand and the duality disappears. Awareness then not only illuminates the object, but creates a space which goes beyond the experience of a limited field. Awareness is transformed from a focused construct to a pervasive space having no location. Awareness not only assumes a new position relative to all objects of experience, but illuminates a larger number of objects than would seem to be possible in ordinary cognitive awareness. It is as though perception of detail is greatly expanded along with an increase in actual capacity to process "information." The "information," however, is no longer divided into cognitive "chunks" and processed sequentially. By way of analogy, we might ordinarily look and see a man sitting on a park bench. In meditation it may be as though we are simultaneously seeing the man on the bench, the tree behind him, a bird on one of its branches, and also are aware of sounds outside and our own bodily sensations, all with greater clarity than the ordinary perception of the man alone.

In the context of this freer space, emotion may be experienced in a very immediate way. We might ordinarily become immersed in vague anger. The usual tendency is to avoid full awareness of the anger. Even forced or impulsive expression can be an avoidance of genuine contact with the feeling. Through becoming the anger, we may become aware of its underlying basis which may be rage directed toward someone we hadn't realized we were angry with. We may then gain insight into fears which blocked awareness of the rage and of whom it was directed against. In this freer space, feelings of attraction and avoidance can be experienced without their causing us to grasp at the positive experiences or run away from, and defend against, the negative ones. The cognitive and affective basis of indifference may unfold, exposing underlying conflicts. In this way, feeling reactions, fears basic to one's character style, and specific phobias can be experienced and accepted with equanimity. The deeply engrained bases of such feeling reactions may, over time, be revealed and replaced with clear awareness.

Another way in which meditation may contribute to growth is by initiating a process of relabeling. Initial reactions to meditative experiences vary greatly. There are sometimes reports of astonishment, shock, uncertainty, and confusion, particularly with an experience of temporary loss of identity or an alteration of space and time. Themes indicative of change and transformation may appear in dreams and fantasy. New emotions and sensations may be experienced in customary social situations. A satisfactory account of what is happening may not be immediately apparent. Ready-made labels and assumptions about ourselves may not apply directly to our experience. Under such conditions Social Comparison Process Theory predicts that a person will reduce uncertainty by seeking explanations of his condition which are subjectively satisfying.[5] Unaccountable experiences may require new assumptions, explanations, and labels. "The more we come to understand what 'mind' is, the more rapidly our conception of 'mind' changes. At first we may think we understand mind, but later, our concepts and labels change."[6]

When topics such as "mind" come under examination in the context of meditation, one's personal cosmology or system for understanding himself, the world, and his relation to the world may very likely be implicated. New insights based on images, memories, symbols, and feelings may emerge as products of meditation and then be evaluated in the context of one's view of himself and the world. It is because such formed products emerge, in part, from outside the everyday conscious point of view, that they are likely to serve as viable input to a growth process. They are less subject to the constraints implicit in one's usual ways of perceiving or constructing the world. Products of meditation, such as a vision of death and afterlife, for example, may be considered material for an assimilative or integrative process and be worked with in any number of ways. Within the context of psychotherapy, for example, such material might serve as the basis for free association in psychoanalysis, amplification in Jungian analysis, or assimilation in Gestalt therapy. Alternatively, such products and associated feelings may undergo transformation within the meditation itself. One's own mind becomes the therapeutic situation and a laboratory for change. Alterations in self-image or personal cosmology, ensuing from an ongoing process of unlabeling, reformulation, and relabeling, may thus become an integral part of a growth process.

The effects of this kind of cognitive reorganization can extend further than having an alternative map with which to view the world. There may be changes in the way we feel that go beyond a purely intellectual reformulation. Interactions between cognitive, affective, and physiological variables have, in general, been confirmed in experimental studies. Several schools of psychotherapy, including George Kelley's Personal Construct Therapy, Albert Ellis' Rational Emotive Therapy, and Attribution Therapy, primarily restructure the client's view of himself and the world with the aim of bringing about more extensive dispositional changes.

If we assume a developmental model, this suggests that changes at the developmentally mature level of abstract cognition could affect the underlying apperceptive process to some extent. For example, if a meditator labeled his state as a "hypnotic trance," developmentally prior functions, such as *kun-gzhi*, would be expected to shift toward heavier densities and narrowed attention consistent with the culturally given meaning of the term "trance." If a state were labeled as an "experience of emptiness," then developmentally prior functions would be lighter and support more spontaneous attention.

Buddhist practices are taught within the context of a comprehensive philosophy and world view which functions to provide a cognitive framework, accommodate advances, and facilitate practice at any level of attainment. The direction of the change process is thus guided, to some extent, by cues provided within the tradition. These cues are, in part, contained in the highly specific experiential meanings of terms such as samsara, nirvana, samadhi, emptiness, form, balance, transmutation, mindfulness, awareness, and even meditation.

As proficiency in meditation and the use of this system develops, we may begin to tune into previously unknown aspects of our inner functioning. We may note, for example, that as our experience changes from moment to moment, all aspects of the apperceptive process change inexplicably. *Kun-gzhi* may be more or less open in different emotional states and in meditation. With recognition of *kun-gzhi rnam-shes* and *yid*, we may directly experience non-cognitive forms of activity and a coming into being of perception and thought. Having developed these insights, it is relatively easy to develop an understanding of self-concept and ego. At this stage of practice, implications for understanding the composition of mental events that we ordinarily assume to be stable, such as our sense of self or identity, may become almost unavoidable. Some fundamental changes in perspective of a sort to be discussed may also occur.

Lama Mi-pham wrote, "After examining and purifying mind . . . finding the absence of a personal self . . . and with certainty of this crucial insight . . . 'I' become the composition of the parts."[7] This "I" is a reference point which, for example, may be formed relative to some kind of "doubt." Both the "I" and the "doubt" may be seen as products of an origination process. "I" may "doubt" that "I" will ever become enlightened. This whole situation poses a "problem." The overall experience of "having a problem" is a composition subject to processes of origination similar to the "I" and the "doubt." The "I" who is having the "problem" is crucial to its survival as are various supporting beliefs. One's capacity for becoming enlightened may be doubted, for example, because of a knowledge that he failed at other significant tasks. All of these mental events are infused with emotion, clustered in a meaningful way, and may be seen to be similarly constituted in a freer pervasive space. It was in this context that Tarthang Tulku once stated that we have problems only because we believe in them and accept their supporting ideas as a part of our predicament. "Like carpenters, we tend to 'shape' our minds, and each of us can shape our mind in a completely different way. We do this mainly by labeling and forming different concepts."[8]

To recognize and know the constituents of constructed mental events such as the "I" or "this problem" in the intrinsic way being discussed, is, at the same time, to go beyond them experientially. It seems unlikely that someone could experience himself, say, as an inherently transient process, or a "composition of the parts" and be at that moment unchanged. Such experiences require an alteration of ego functioning. The question, "Who is doing the thinking?" is at this point no longer a purely intellectual exercise. Direct experience may provide some astonishing insights into the nature of one's existence. One possible outcome of direct experience is a realization that the formed units of experience which we ordinarily accept as being real, including our own identity, have "no basis."

For myself, I can recall my utter disbelief, skepticism, and sense of awe during several months of rapid change. My astonishment seemed not to be based on various altered states of perception which I experienced during that period. I had by then learned to allow any "fantastic vision" to come and go like water under a bridge. Far more shocking and meaningful was the realization that regardless of the mundane or the extraordinary quality of an experience, there was nothing which could be located except in relation to something else. Nothing could be found with a permanent place, including myself, and nothing in the entirety of existence could be seen to have any basis other than its own existence. Words such as "transient" and "insubstantial" can only be used to summarize the implications which experiences beyond description have for the solid world in which "I" has some real meaning.

Along with these perspectives comes some freedom from constraints normally imposed by cognition, emotion, and the structure of inner experience. Knowing the insubstantial nature of the observing "I," thoughts, feelings, or whatever, we can go beyond, in front of, behind, or within these constructions and choose to act outside of the illusory constraints. It is with this realization that a new dimension of freedom becomes available. Choice and personal change is possible because there is nothing in us that is substantial and permanent.

Even with a high degree of proficiency and insight in meditation, having undergone significant change, we may still find ourselves involved in samsara. Our desires and fears may be in some perspective, but still they become manifest in new ways. Unaware, we find ourselves grasping, running, attacking, and still dissatisfied. Our presence of mind is incomplete. In the commentary on Lama Mi-pham's work it is said:

> The fictions of mind, the fantasies which have been mistaken for the genuine reality remain to colour the vision in ways that obscure it. These are deeply ingrained habits of perception, insisting that somewhere there is a fundamental distinction between 'I' and 'it', between subject and object, between the poles of every duality.[8]

Tarthang Tulku also emphasized that even in advanced stages of practice, these ingrained habits of perception or "residues" arise out of *kun-gzhi*. These "residues" continually emerge from the store consciousness in new forms which capture our fascination. Engrained habits of perception may be removed as they take form by means of full mindfulness. Meditation ideally becomes an unbroken awareness which is not withdrawn with the occurrence of cognitive and emotional snags which, through capturing the focus of attention, limit a broader awareness and full presence of mind. To carry this unbroken awareness into everyday life is one objective of Buddhist practice. Gradually an awareness which is intrinsic, alive to the moment, and which does not stop to fixate on form, may develop.

Although action will still be within samsara, the cyclical patterning of our behavior may be less compulsive and blind. Ordinary action is on the basis of emotional preference and abstract thought. While ignoring neither, a healthy meditative attitude rests on a commitment to awareness and full realization. It is continuity of awareness which provides the means of overcoming most obstacles. When fully realized, awareness is both the means of realization and the goal. Awareness goes beyond the level of differentiated cognition and adequate ego functioning to original awareness, responsive and spontaneous action, boundless compassion, and presence of mind that sees its own ignorance, pain, happiness, and folly. There is freedom to accept or reject the manifestations of samsaric mind with equanimity.

Notes:

1. Tarthang Tulku, "On Thoughts," *Crystal Mirror* (1974) 3:9–10.

2. Tarthang Tulku, "The Self-Image," *Crystal Mirror* (1974) 3:32–40.

3. Lama Mi-pham, *Calm and Clear* (Berkeley: Dharma Publishing, 1973), p. 108.

4. Tarthang Tulku, "On Thoughts," pp. 12–13.

5. L. Festinger, "A Theory of Social Comparison Processes," *Human Relations* (1954) 7:117–40.

6. Tarthang Tulku, "Mind and Feelings," *Crystal Mirror* (1974) 3:77.

7. Lama Mi-pham, *Calm and Clear*, p. 101.

8. Tarthang Tulku, "Mind and Feelings," p. 77.

9. Lama Mi-pham, *Calm and Clear*, p. 102.

Wholesomeness: Approaches to Diagnostic Assessment

Kendra Smith

When a person seeks help for emotional or interpersonal problems at a clinic, a "diagnostic work-up" is done preliminary to drawing up a "treatment plan." The purpose is to determine how this particular person can best be helped to change his outlook or behavior. A Buddhist teacher also makes psychological assessments of the pupils who come to him seeking inner change, in order to give them practices suitable to their condition, or to help them with obstacles in their meditation practice. Although the clinic patient seeks insight and the Buddhist aspirant seeks enlightenment, a comparison is possible. Each seeks a way out of suffering

KENDRA SMITH holds a Ph.B. from the University of Chicago and has worked widely as a psychiatric social worker. She has received training in organizational development from N.T.L.–U.C.L.A. Graduate School of Business and in family therapy from Boston Family Institute. She is a graduate of the 1974 Human Development Training Program.

through an understanding of, and a change in, his mind and emotions. Mental health professionals can also be seen as the counterparts of Buddhist teachers since they have largely supplanted priests as counsellors and spiritual guides in modern Western society.

Western clinical psychology, like Buddhism, begins with the fact of suffering, the first of the Noble Truths, and with the questions: "What are the roots of suffering?" and "What is the way out?"

The roots of suffering, in the Buddhist view, are ignorance and the illusion of a separate and stable Ego, an illusion that is the product of mind that construes an unrealistic wall between the organism and all with which the organism is in exchange. The result of this illusion is fear of the outer world that has been artificially created by mind, a world which is perceived as something which must be cajoled or dominated, and a continual agonizing checking, comparing the illusory self with others perceived to be separate and in opposition to the vulnerable Ego.

By contrast, most Western psychology suggests that the distinction between Ego and Other can hardly be made too clear-cut. "Magical thinking" and other distortions are assumed to be the result of a porous or "Swiss cheese" ego. The difference is not simply a semantic one, I think, but rests on the Western conviction that the Ego or Self is a fixed entity which changes only adaptively, like a water skier shifting his body to ride the waves.

In Freudian psychology the cause of ordinary mental suffering is frustration which comes from clashes between appetitive impulses and societal restrictions internalized as superego and guilt feelings. Exceptional mental suffering stems from a too punishing superego and an unrealistic ego-ideal, which produces anxiety and symptoms which are a crippling, ineffective response to the anxiety. The psychoanalytic view seems to imply that the substitutions and sublimations of appetitive pleasures are never quite as blissful as the original sensual gratifications. The closest thing to paradise in this view is the well-satisfied baby. Adults therefore must live on a substratum of melancholy because life in civilized groups requires much repression of our appetitive cravings.

Buddhism, rather than equating happiness with the complete and immediate satisfaction of all appetitive needs, notes the compulsivity involved in meeting even the most ordinary needs—feeding and clothing oneself—and points the way to freedom from cravings and aversions. Bliss is not seen as the property of infancy but as the result of realizing a nonseparate self in which consciousness is not an entity but a continuous coming into being and dying away. Joy, compassion, and awareness are seen as natural, possible conditions for man. And when the Buddhist teacher makes psychological assessments, he positions the pupil in his progress toward this awakening. Western psychology, although it struggles to find a consensually acceptable model of health, has in everyday practice only a negative definition of health: freedom from gross pathological symptoms. Conceptually, the Western practitioner is almost blind to health.

My interest in this issue has a history. The fascination with why people are the way they are, which led me to my vocational choice, included wonder and interest in why some people are so qualitatively different from others. Even a brief meeting with some persons seems to leave a small light within one, a place of refuge. My mind goes to one example, Wm. Ernest Hocking, who was one of America's most respected philosophers early in this century. I had the chance to meet him when he was past ninety years of age, living alone atop a New Hampshire mountain. Most of his colleagues, family, and friends were gone, his fame and influence were in eclipse, but he was translucent with joy. With tender gaiety he related as readily to some children as to a fellow philosopher, and without self-conscious or well-intentioned fumbling. The maples and pines, the beavers damming his stream, the clouds sweeping over the peaks, the piano on which he played a duet

with a child—he seemed in the same I-Thou relationship with them all. I know no English word for the tuned-in quality of awareness which I sensed in Hocking, and have sensed in Zen roshis, and in others.

We could say that Hocking was a Bodhisattva. Western psychology has no concept of Bodhisattvahood, and holds no promise of nor method for such attainment. Erik Erikson comes closest when he describes the potential that is inherent in the eight stages of the life cycle, particularly the potential for attaining "generativity" and "integrity" in the latter part of life when the individual sense of identity can transcend the narrow boundaries of selfhood and expand, affirmatively, beyond the limits of culture to include all human beings who came before and all who will come after.

Although the assessment of "ego strengths" is given lip service, Western diagnostic procedures and tools are, like a surgeon's scalpel, designed to uncover only pathology. Both Buddhism and Western psychologists feel that it is essential for patient or aspirant to be motivated and to take responsibility for his growth, but Buddhist psychology accords more importance to the Virtues as antidotes to the forces (greed, stupidity, and illusion) which perpetuate neurotic suffering. "Wholesome factors of consciousness," like mindfulness, selflessness, detachment, shame, sympathy, etc., are valued, like money in the bank, a hedge against karmic debt. Never do these factors—and rarely do the courage, humor, and idealism so movingly apparent in many patients—appear in the buff-colored sheets titled "Diagnostic Summary."

In the clinic I would occasionally come across a child or adult who stood out from the rest of his family and environment, relatively unscathed, it seemed, by the distortions and misery around him, and I would wonder how it happened. The standard explanations were all negative: (1) the person who had escaped obvious pathology despite all professional expectations had done so because he was not singled out by the parents to be scapegoat, or to be the object of their negative identification; or (2) the apparent healthy functions were compensations for ego defects lurking below the surface, like geological faults beneath the earth's crust which become devouring earthquakes when enough stress accumulates.

It is dogma in Western psychology that one cannot escape the negative influences of early childhood conditioning except through psychoanalysis or other therapies. Buddhist psychology, too, asserts an inexorable relationship between thought and action and its effect in samsaric existence. However, discrepancies between childhood situation and adult produced are neatly avoided by the assumption that the causal chain reaches back into the karmic accumulation of lifetimes, not just one childhood. Perhaps the vicissitudes of weaning and potty training (viewed as critical expressions of the parent-child relationship) which have preoccupied Western psychologists were ignored by the builders of Buddhist psychology because the latter lived in static and homogeneous cultures; Nāgārjuna, for example, may have had little chance to ponder the differential effects of different child-rearing practices. But even if he had, it seems likely that he would have remained more impressed with the similarities in human existence which give rise to suffering, than with the effects of different parental styles.

Whenever it was possible, I began to study those persons I found in whom childhood experience and adult capacities were not obvious continuities. Especially interesting were those rare ones who seemed to have transmuted harsh childhood experiences into exceptional sensitivity and compassion, like the proverbial lotus growing out of slime. One of these was a young woman I will call Karas.

Over a period of three years I saw Karas in a variety of situations, and also met her family. She agreed to be a subject for a dozen or more interviews and to take a battery of psychological tests given by a staff psychologist at the mental health clinic where I worked.

Karas was in an encounter group for students which I led in a wilderness cabin. Her energy, exuberance, and openness moved the group forward in its psychological work, and also helped to get the communal meals cooked and the necessary cleaning up accomplished in good spirits. Her quick but friendly wit and her sensitivity to the vulnerability of others enormously influenced the group's cohesion and norms.

The next year Karas was a member of a student group

with which I travelled around the world for an academic year
to study utopian ideas and communities. Thirty-eight Americans, moving rapidly from country to country in lockstep, we
felt as though we were canned together in a submarine. An in-
group and an out-group emerged, nerves frayed and snapped;
yet by the end of the year we felt that we had found utopia,
that through trial and effort we had become "the beloved
community." Again the traits in Karas that had done so much
for the encounter group contributed substantially to this
happy ending.

During this travel year I began to learn about the psycho-
pathology in her family and the difficulties of her growing up;
but before summarizing those, a few vignettes from the travel
year will make the person more real. Following a week-long
stay in a Zen monastery, arranged for all students who wished
it, Karas on her own sought out a Zen temple where she could
continue to practice daily *zazen,* and she persisted even
though panic-feelings and nausea arose during her meditation. India was the high point of her year's trip. Here she went
from Delhi to Dharamsala to visit Tibetans near the Dalai
Lama's residence in exile, a courageous undertaking for a
young woman alone. She returned happy and aglow from her
first contact with Tibetan Sangha—and also with cracked,
slightly bloody feet because she had given all of her socks to
the refugee monks, whose need, in their mountain tents, was
greater than her own.

An incident with some street gypsies in Macedonia shows
her playful gaiety. After making overtures to one of the gypsy
babies, which caused the infant to erupt in delighted gurgles,
Karas snatched the baby up and pretended to run off.
The gypsies, outcasts defamed as baby-stealers, shouted with
laughter at this teasing reminder of their reputation. Next
Karas admired a young gypsy woman's jewelry, and learned
how her hair was braided with yarn, and how her full harem
pants were constructed, all through sign language and much
laughter. Somehow it was decided that the two would ex-

change clothes, Karas putting on the necklaces and full gathered pants, the young gypsy donning faded American levis and Radcliffe sweat shirt. The women—gypsies and two Americans—held out blankets to screen the two while they made the exchange of clothing, while gypsy men, beyond the circle of blankets, expressed ribald glee.

On her return to the U.S. Karas found a house in the country, organized a commune, planted a large vegetable garden, got a job with a welfare department, and began saving her wages for a return to India and Dalhousie. In her job she effectively organized a cooperative day-care center in a slum area of disorganized families, and showed exceptional sensitivity and concern in the crises that came up. Because of her concern she considered giving up her plan to return to India, but the day-care center was going well, and she returned. Letters—lyrical, amusing, and reflective—came, with pictures of young tulkus to whom she gave chocolate brownies along with English lessons; a report of a workshop in *vipassanā* meditation; and an account of her trek to Everest. Two young American men with whom Karas had started the climb dropped out after two days, but Karas persisted all the way to base camp, wearing a cotton dress and tennis shoes, stopping at night in tiny villages where she would ask if she might cook her barley over a family's fire and share their floor space to spread a sleeping bag.

It was during her work year in the U.S. that the interviews and psychological testing took place. The earliest thing Karas could recall was being restricted in her crib for long hours, watching the shadows move, warned by her mother to be quiet so her father would not become agitated. From these early years Karas believed her father to be unstable, and her mother stronger but a victim. However, despite her belief in her father's violence, it turned out that she had never actually known him to do anything more violent than throw a jar of pickles on the floor. He was away and in a mental hospital for about a year when Karas was four.

As a baby Karas was bottle-fed. Her mother explained when Karas asked years later, "My milk was bad." Her mother also said of Karas, "You were born contented, but you have been discontented ever since." When Karas was ten to eleven, her mother began to work at a job that required travel, and Karas was required to take over the housework and younger siblings. At about this time she began to have bleeding colitis.

The family moved repeatedly, but Karas was able to form relationships, two of them with surrogate-mothers, important though shortlived. The first, when she was five or six, was with a Sunday school teacher who taught her about Jesus. The figure of Jesus, watching over, loving, and approving her work, sustained Karas through the mountains of housework later and in other times of sorrow. Her parents were not religious, but Karas had a strong interest in religion from these early years through to her study of religion in college.

The many family homes were either in small towns or in the country, and running free in the woods was the happiest part of childhood. Always Karas planted and grew things, and in turn felt befriended by plants and trees. The parental relationship bore heavily on the children. Each parent sought battle allies in the children, and used the children as intermediaries during the months when the parents were angrily refusing to speak directly to each other. Karas accepted her mother's picture of her father as violent and improvident, and felt she should protect her; yet, she had received more affection from her father, so she was sorely conflicted.

Karas related that her mother had been forced to work because of the father's failure to provide, and that she had put herself through Radcliffe College on scholarships and almost full-time employment because her parents were unable to give financial help. I was startled, therefore, to visit the family home, and to find that it was an elegant, flawlessly furnished Colonial overlooking a lake, with several new cars in the driveway. One of them was a shiny new sports car given to

Karas's sister, two years younger, a severely schizoid girl who was hospitalized for several months during the year of our interviews. A brother, slightly older than Karas, appears to have been severely disturbed as a child (e.g., torturing animals). During the interviews I noticed how difficult it was for Karas to deal with painful memories. She would become cloudy and restless, have memory lapses, and illogically jump to some happier memory. With material one might expect would evoke anger, she would justify and excuse her parents before any anger came to expression. During this year she had periods of utter exhaustion and ailments which seemed to have no organic basis. When I wondered if memory-dredging might be the cause, Karas said no, that she wanted to continue with the interviews and that her ailments and weight fluctuations were an old pattern.

As Karas spun out her story the templates of my psychological training fell into their nosological slots—oral deprivation, oral conflict, oral depression; denial, repression, somatization; sado-masochistic parental marriage; mother: character disorder, castrating, dubious reality testing; father: passive-dependent, etc., etc., in the whole dreary litany of diagnostic language.

Nevertheless I was not prepared for the report of the psychologist who gave Karas a Rorschach, a TAT (Thematic Apperception Test), and some other projective tests (e.g., "draw your family"). Karas, he told me, had walked into his office and put her Japanese flute down on his desk.

"It's a phallic symbol, and she has some identity confusion," he said, "but the real issues are oral. Because of her orality, she was trying to excite my interest with an exotic object."

"Oh, she was on her way to a lesson with her Japanese music teacher," I explained. "She has no car, so she was carrying it with her."

This did not influence his interpretation of the incident.

His picture was one of unmitigated pathology, of "ego fragility."

"Yes," I said, "I see pretty much the same things. But what else do you see? How do you account for the fact that she is dealing more creatively with her life than you might expect, given her history. Don't you feel that her intelligence, her gift for expression and reflection enable her to use her experiences more creatively—perhaps in her job, where she has been really innovative?

"Oh yes, I know she is intelligent, so I didn't bother to test her," he responded.

I continued to wonder if he could help me to understand the origin of positive traits. "I know that religious ideas in patients often express guilt or sadism, but in Karas it seems as though it was a corrective emotional experience. It's given her some feeling of meaning and worth, and it's drawing her back to India."

"Flight! Sooner or later she is going to have to face the fact that her problems are internal and stop running. All these kids going to India...," the psychologist sighed. "Look, you like her. It is hard for you to be objective."

This was a typical, well-trained clinical psychologist. How might a Buddhist spiritual tracher, perhaps one who had spent as many years in training as the psychologist had spent in graduate school and internships, have conducted a diagnostic work-up?

There is an assumption in Buddhism that you can only know and help others to the extent that you have developed awareness and compassion, and understand the nature of your own mind. The heart of Buddhist training is the practice of mindfulness and meditation, which develops a finer and finer awareness of the workings of the mind. The awareness which results seems evident in teachers like the Tibetan Rinpoche, Tarthang Tulku, who over and over during the summer seminar I participated in spoke directly to our condition. The way his remarks or questions bore precisely on

The Nyingma Institute, founded in 1973 as a center for conveying the benefits of Tibetan Buddhism's psychological and philosophical insights to the West, became a forum for a dynamic exchange of views and ideas.

thoughts or feelings in the group or in the head of the individual to which they were addressed suggested abilities that seem uncanny to us. It seemed that every remark and bit of information from us, every fleeting look of interest or boredom or perplexity, must have registered and have been intuitively integrated, and instantaneously available without any grinding of computer-mind. He was, moreover, able to be spontaneous and playful without threat to his objectivity or the clarity of his perception. Even his jokes seemed to be both "teaching" and diagnostic techniques. They were projective tests, or a kind of mild confrontation.

The idea of unconscious mental activity, we have generally

assumed, was first formulated by Freud. We know also that it was demonstrated in quantifiable terms by experimental work with tachistoscopes and electric shock equipment and instruments measuring Galvanic Skin Response and pupil dilation. It deflates our Occidental *hubris* to learn that centuries ago, without electrodes and kymographic needles, the early Buddhists traced the emergence of any thought or perception through seventeen stages, of which only the last two stages are what is ordinarily called conscious. In the notion of *manas* they conceptualized unconscious motivational systems, which determine what is brought to consciousness, what is ignored, repressed, or denied.

The Buddhist teacher, therefore, presumably would not be oblivious of Karas's defense mechanisms, her somatization, nor the underlying *kleśas* (i.e., emotional conflicts). A conflict, however, would not be understood as it is in the West, as a conflict between id or ego and superego, but more like something which interrupts the smooth flow of appropriate responses, like a knot in a sewing thread. From a Buddhist viewpoint the conflict results from a static, and therefore outdated, definition of self and other.

The Buddhist attitude toward emotional conflicts and defense mechanisms would also be subtly different. As Tarthang Rinpoche put it in answering a question in class, Tibetan Buddhists recognize the distortion of projection, which we label paranoia, but, he said, in Tibet they have no such label which tends to make paranoia an entity, something set apart, a sickness, rather than simple recognition that this too is a way samsaric mind works.

A Tibetan Vajrayāna practitioner would not "take a history" with attention to the early psychosexual stages. Although he might ask Karas a few questions about her family, his questions would be directed to understanding how she deals with negative emotions *now*, how forgiving and open-hearted she is; how she deals with sexuality; which vital energy centers are open and which blocked. He would observe whether she was tense, restless, relaxed, energetic, or torpid. Perhaps more intuitively than analytically, he would note the way she held her body, the areas which were held stiffly or constricted, which parts seemed disowned—much as the practitioners of our newer body therapies would.

The counterpart of the psychologist's projective tests might be a request to report on the nature of the thoughts, images, and sensations which arose during her meditation. He might ask her to observe how her self-images manifest themselves over a period of time, recognizing that she had the intellectual capacity to do this usefully. He might ask her directly about her fears, aversions, attachments, beliefs, and even her sense perceptions.

Mental phenomena of little interest to the Western psychologist would be of central importance to the Buddhist in evaluating wholesome factors of consciousness (i.e., those which are conducive to Enlightenment). First among these would be intelligence, which in Karas is quick and subtle, comprehending and expressive, an "alertness and pliability of mind and body." Nearly equal in importance would be Karas's enthusiastic and steady engagement in the Path, her persistence in meditation despite the "emotions which are robbers of attention and effort," and which in Karas's meditation manifested themselves as nausea and a strangling panic.

It would be wrong to regard the Vajrayāna teacher's interest in a capacity for poetic expression or compassionate feeling as soft-hearted sentimentality. He may be as capable of going straight to the site of trouble as a dentist's drill, but he would also see the interrelatedness of a very broad range of phenomena. Karas's wish to return to India, and her spiritual interests would not be dismissed as flight from internal problems.

There are other traits of Karas which would be noted as indicative of wholesome *dharmas*: her lightness and "active implementation of joy," as in the characteristic play with the gypsies; her sympathy and compassion (as expressed in her

work and gift of her socks in Dalhousie) which is an antidote
to aversion; her joy in the contemplation of beauty, which is a
temporary loss of egohood and an antidote to grasping; the
purity of her right speech and right livelihood; her care not to
hurt nor harm; her freedom from rigid or dogmatic reliance
on rules and rituals; her intellectual comprehension of the
concepts of *anicca* and *anatta* (the doctrines of "the change
and transitoriness in all things," and "no separate, endur-
ing self").

Rather than assigning Karas to one of the categories of
neurosis or character disorder (the inevitable result of diagnostic procedure in the West where there is no model of
positive health as reference point), she would be identified as
belonging to one of nine psychological types. These categories
refer to the way in which the aspirant learns and responds, and
denote which teachings and practices would be most beneficial in helping him to awaken from illusion and ignorance. A
Buddhist teacher might identify Karas as a *sotāpanna*, "one
who has entered the stream," and therefore as a member of
one of the four classes of "noble individuals" (*ariyapuggala*).

Both Eastern and Western psychology agree on existential
suffering, and there are many similarities in the way they
understand mind; yet there is a great gulf, which accounts
for how the Western psychologist described here could see
only a delusionary escapist in a young woman who could be
called a *sotāpanna*. There are at least two important reasons
for this gulf: differences of methodology; and the concept of
anatta, or no real, persistent ego entity. Language, too, at least
for English-speaking persons, may be an obstacle to bridging
the gulf. English deals more handily with abstract concepts
than some languages which are more concrete, I'm told, but at
the same time it reifies concepts, making entities of what
more accurately are functional-relationships-in-process-in-a-
network-of-systems.

Western thought, influenced by modern physics, is moving
away from what Buddhism would call dualism. Western

science is more and more cognizant that what filters through our sensory apparatus and through our conceptualizing, programmed brains is not "reality" in any but a relative sense. More and more, Western science is demonstrating the interrelatedness of all things. And yet it is very hard for us to entertain the Buddhist idea that our individual consciousness is only a discontinuous stream of perpetual perishing and arising, and that what we regard as a stable, familiar, persevering Self is simply a trick of our memory functions, an illusion. Yet there is precedence for acceptance of *anatta* even in Western psychology. Harry Stack Sullivan wrote in the thirties that the idea of individual self was a "heuristic construct." His notion of the self was rather like the myth of Indra's net, in which each reflecting node in the net represented a relationship, which also reflected every other human relationship. However, his theory of personality has been neglected in our graduate schools although his innovative methods for treating schizophrenia remain influential.

Differences in methodology are the greatest gulf between Eastern and Western psychology. Psychology in the West calls itself a behavioral science and subscribes to the canons of science. A psychology oriented toward Enlightenment, which cannot be consensually validated nor measured nor operationally defined will be rejected as unscientific. Because no other way of knowing enjoys as much status in the West, academic psychology has turned itself inside out trying to fit the model of the pre-Einsteinian natural sciences. Because human behavior eludes quantification, prediction, and control, there has been a heavy reliance on probability equations, correlation coefficients, averages, the "test of significance," and the law of large numbers. This virtually rules out study of the exceptional and supranormal, which is intrinsic to Buddhist psychology with its goal of developing qualitatively different states of being.

This brings us back to the earlier comparison of Eastern and Western methods of assessing wholesome and unwholesome factors of consciousness (Buddhist) and/or personality (clinical). American psychologists can seem like antibodies that feed on purulence, who rush to the site of infection, ignoring what is wholesome. Does this attitude and expectation work to increase dysfunction? The Buddhist teacher, with Enlightenment as his horizon, looks for those factors of consciousness which move the person away from grasping and illusion, for those "undefiled *dharmas*" which permit the person to discern the results of his thoughts and actions more finely. Perhaps this attitude is in itself more health-giving.

Self-Image

Peggy Lippitt

In the West we have been taught to look at life as if separateness were reality. We think of life dualistically—as subject and object, good and bad, you and me. At the core of Buddhist philosophical thought is the concept that, in reality, there is no separated self. Relinquishing the idea of the separated self or ego is a state to be diligently cultivated on the path to enlightenment.

To us the idea of *no self* comes as a shock. Many of us in teaching or other helping professions have spent the better part of our lives encouraging children to develop strong egos. We have taught other people how to help children meet those

PEGGY LIPPITT holds an M.A. in Education from U.C.L.A. She has served as Project Director of the Cross-Age Helping Program at the University of Michigan, Founder and Director of The Children, Youth, and Family Laboratory for the National Training Laboratories, and as a senior staff member of Human Resources Development Associates of Ann Arbor, Michigan.

"ego integrative needs" we deemed so necessary for building a healthy identity. What have we been doing all these years? Have we been totally off the beam? Or is it necessary to the effective functioning in this world to think of yourself as separate before you can become aware of your oneness with all life?

In meditation one gradually becomes aware, one contacts awareness. At that moment, you are contacting your own mind nature, and in realizing the contact, you are no longer separate. No subject, no object, no separation. Your mind, your awareness are one. However, without some experience that gives you this certainty about the oneness of life, it may seem strange to be told that the separated self is "unreal." This is particularly so since we operate so much of the time as if being separate selves were the only way of being.

The philosopher Descartes was characteristically Western when he stated, "I think, therefore I am." Very soon in our summer program of Buddhist studies we had experiences that undermined this attitude. One of our first assignments was to observe our thoughts. It was easy to distinguish between the observer and the thought. We could also be aware of ourselves as the observer apart from and independent of the thoughts we were observing. We were not existing because we had thoughts. Our thoughts existed because we thought them.

Tarthang Rinpoche often talked about thoughts. He said they are tools, and, as such, are very useful. They can generate more thoughts. They can produce emotions, channel energy, cause action and experience. But they are limited. They cannot make discoveries.

I was struck with the similarity of this to what Robert Pirsig says in *Zen and the Art of Motorcycle Maintenance* about the scientific method in problem solving. "It is good for seeing where you have been, but it can't tell you where you ought to go unless where you ought to go is a continuation of where you were going in the past. Creativity, originality, inventiveness, intuition and imagination are completely out of its domain."[1]

Self-image as a thought

Our next assignment in the area of "thought watching" was to observe our self-image. Let me clarify further what is meant by self-image by quoting from an article by Tarthang Tulku on this subject.

Self-image is interesting, because when we examine it, it doesn't show itself. It cannot be pinpointed as anything. You may have concepts about a certain self-image you may have at a particular time, but there is no *one* particular self-image that *outlasts* any conceptions you may have about it.

We think and talk as if we could actually touch and see our self-image. What is important to understand is that there are actually two separate qualities acting: our 'self' or 'me' or 'I' and our self-image. This 'me' or 'I' is involved with life in a multitude of ways. This 'I ' experiences and feels and sees things in a way which is very much alive, very immediate. But when this 'I' becomes imbued with the self-image, the person is not really himself—he is acting as if he were some other person. For example, you are tremendously shy, or you feel very shameful, embarrassed or guilty. At this time the 'I' is overcome with a very vivid, very alive sensation which is really only the activation of the self-image. Two separate things are occurring. The first is the operation of the five skandhas or 'elements' which make up the human being. But apart from these there is an additional force which is the self-image.

We can think, examine-meditate and maybe make very clear to ourselves, what kind of status we are giving to this self-image. Let us say you are watching your thoughts and emotions during some tremendous disturbance, some great sadness. Your mind is very agitated. At these times you might be able to observe that you are not actually the person who is experiencing this emotional state. You are not the one who is creating those disturbances. They are being created through the operation of your self-image. But sometimes this is hard to see because you are so involved with the self-image you have created throughout your life. What is essential for you to see is that, during those particularly painful disturbances, you have the opportunity to step back and actually see the core of your self-image. For instance, when certain energies develop—a trembling or volcanic sort of consciousness, or a feeling of fear, or anger, or tightness—what is creating this *holding strength* is the self-image.

But just like the self-image, this holding strength does not really exist. Just as there is no abiding 'self' or 'ego' there is no abiding self-image. True, the actual feeling is there, but its holding power will be completely lost as soon as you have lost your interest in feeding the self-image. At that time you can have a totally different experience than what you had thought was possible in that previous state of painfulness.

It is so easy to let the self-image perpetuate itself, dominate your whole life, and create an unbalanced state of affairs. . . . How can we involve ourselves less with our self-image, and how can we make ourselves more flexible? We are human beings, not animals, and we do not have to live as if we were in cages or in bondage. At the present level, before we start meditating on the self-image, we do not realize the difference between our self-image and our 'self'. We do not have an access-gate or point of departure. But if we can recognize just some small difference between our self-image and ourself or 'I' or 'me', we can then see which part is the self-image.[2]

Tarthang Rinpoche asked us to look for our self-images wherever we could find them, in and out of meditation. This assignment lasted two weeks. For me it was very fruitful.

The Lama made it easier for us to spot our self-images by suggesting questions to investigate: "How are you and your self-image related?" "Do you belong to your personality or does your personality belong to you?" "Look carefully at the back of restlessness and emotional feelings. What is there?"

He also gave us helpful advice: "Let the door open; accept it. Look at it even if you don't like to do it or see it. If you don't like it, kill it. It has no life. It is only a thought. . . ." By this he meant that when we discovered a self-image we didn't like, we didn't have to give it any more energy: "Its holding power will be completely lost as soon as we have lost interest in feeding it." Deprived of energy to keep it alive, the thought form that

Lotus in bloom — ancient symbol of awakened mind.

was the self-image will fade away into thin air like the Cheshire cat in *Alice's Adventures in Wonderland*. The energy which we had heretofore directed into preserving the self-image will then be available to us for more useful purposes.

With reference to this resource of reclaimed energy one has at one's disposal, Tarthang Rinpoche said, "Positive and negative self-images are each of value. Both carry energy that can be used. The worst thing has energy. It is very valuable." (This was a particularly poignant statement for me as I have never had much tolerance for imperfection in myself or others.)

He gave us further assurance: "The personality and the energy can be transformed." "Clean up inside and you'll feel better. Lose your self-image, and then you will have a much better time, be more compassionate and flexible." Thus supported, I began the search.

First I had to identify what I was looking for. Some definitions for the self-image which I found useful were: A self-image is a thought about or belonging to any aspect of the separated self as apart from the One Life. These include any subject-object thought in connection with me, for example: "I am better than he is (or worse)." "I must get into the top group." Any grasping, wanting, manipulating, or clinging thought about the separated self is also in the category of self-image, for example: "I want to be in the limelight." "I want things my way." Or, "I want you to act thus and so."

Self-image can be a type of *fixation*. It catches you, and you freeze there. You accept the static, frozen image as a true and permanent picture of yourself. For example, a little girl comes to believe girls are no good. She thinks: "I am a girl. Therefore, I am no good."

Next I needed to define *me* so I wouldn't get mixed up with my self-image. In Christianity it is said, "I am a member of Christ, a child of God, an inheritor of the Kingdom of Heaven." That is comforting. But it makes me feel impotent and dependent against God's omnipotence.

Let's try again. How about "I am a partner with God"? I have always loved Robert Browning's poem about Antonio Stradivarius, the great Italian violin maker. In it Stradivarius speaks as follows, 'If my hand slacks I leave a blank where violins should be. . . . How can God make Stradivarius violins without Antonio?" But this is still a separated concept of the self—God and I.

Here's another definition I have used in times past. "I am soul." But "soul" is a concept that implies perfection. I don't know how to deal with my imperfections as "soul." And then, too, it is possible to give soul a connotation of separateness: your soul, my soul, his soul, etc. No, that won't do either.

There is a story about the trainer of the famous movie dog, Rin-Tin-Tin. He was trying to describe this beautiful animal to a friend. No adjective he could think of seemed quite adequate to capture the quality he was trying to convey. Finally he came up with this definition: "Rin-Tin-Tin," he said, "is dignity manifesting as a dog." This led me to a definition of myself which seemed flexible enough and clear enough for present purposes—to wit: "I am the One Life, manifesting as Peggy."

Armed with this definition of "me," I began tracking down my elusive self-images.

Some discoveries

Having accepted the fact that it is all right to have "bad" self-images and that imperfect self-images are useful holders of energy that could be transmuted and redirected, it was easier to open the door to them. And they, for their part, felt less guilty about showing themselves. I began to keep a list of every thought I could identify about me as a separated self. Here are some examples: "I need to be *the best*, the favorite, etc." "I don't want to tackle things when I'm not at my best. I'm prideful." "I fear failure." "I want to be the top of the class; the princess, nothing less." "I deny what I don't like and pretend it doesn't exist."

A lot of these, I discovered, were how my self-image made me feel or think rather than being the self-image itself. Sometimes the self-image is harder to find than the thoughts and feelings it generates.

I was interested and amused to discover how many of my thoughts about myself were on the order of, "I like so and so. But I do wish he'd wash his hair!" This self-image surely wants to change people, I thought with an inward chuckle.

I found a lot of my self-images wanted to boss: "That's not the right way to set a table!" Many were competitively oriented: "I'm not as good as" or "I'm better than so-and-so." Some wanted power or possessions: "If only he'd listen to me."

Some showed themselves more clearly at certain ages. At

eleven I remember I had a great desire for a dog. But I got no joy from owning a dog of questionable breeding. My self-image demanded a thoroughbred, pedigreed dog to satisfy it. Some self-images were frightened ones. Sometimes the fright hid a feeling of worthlessness. Sometimes it was a mask for pride. "I'm afraid to do this for fear it won't be perfect, and whatever I do *has* to be perfect." Or, "If I continue on this line of thought, I'll discover something I'd rather not know about myself."

From time to time during the two weeks we worked on this assignment, Rinpoche would give us further hints about how to catch our self-images and to understand them. One way was to go to what he called a "density" emotional state; a wrathful state or one of frustration or depression. Wait there, letting the self-image come up. It's like waiting to catch a fish. Look! It's rising! Still, now. Watch how it takes control, initiates action. When it's once out in the open enough to watch what it is doing, you can usually hook it.

Some self-images don't want to be found. They have interesting, invisible ways of discouraging the seeker. You can see this happening when you catch yourself thinking, "Forget it. It doesn't make sense." Where does this resistance come from? Maybe another self-image is lurking close to the surface.

I thought one exercise we did was very useful in helping to unearth buried self-images. We were asked to go back over our whole lives, time period by time period, to see if we could discover certain recurring patterns of behavior. In this way we could perhaps locate the self-images *responsible* for adopting these recurring behaviors. Then we could get a toehold on how we could change these behavior patterns, if we wanted to. Find the self-images that generated the action. Just let them go. Let them fade away. Some people believe that after death we are given a chance like this to re-evaluate the events of our lives in terms of seeable cause and effect patterns. Few of us have a chance to do this while there is still time to take

advantage of our findings in our lifetime. It was an exciting
opportunity, but not always pleasant. However, the more
dreadful the self-image one unearthed, the greater the relief
when it was consciously looked at and "done away with."
Although one reached into very painful areas one had been
hiding from conscious awareness, the greater the immediate
pain, the greater the subsequent joy of becoming free from
that cage. Even so, this sort of self-investigation takes forti-
tude. It reminded me of Amelia Earhart's definition of courage: "The price that life exacts for granting peace."

Not all my self-images were negative, by any means. Some
were positive, indeed. But negative or positive, it didn't seem
to make much difference now that I knew they were only
thoughts to which I had become attached, thoughts which had
no reality in themselves.

It was even often hard to tell whether they were positive or
negative. What mattered, I saw, was that when you have such
images and don't know it, they will dictate your actions. When
you know them as self-images, you can become free from such
dictation. You can act with awareness of what is appropriate
at the moment rather than from habit or some computer-
ized response that one of your self-images has fed into the
control system.

One case in point occurred during the summer program
when I was asked to give help in a way for which I had no
skills. Previously I would have been compelled to live up to
my "good" self-image as a helper by saying that I would.
Instead I wondered if my self-image as a helper was indeed
"good." Maybe it came from another self-image which por-
trayed me as "not so good" and said, "I have to be a helper in
order to be accepted," and from still another that said, "I
desire more than anything else to be accepted." I considered it
a small turning point in my ability to be inner-directed that in
this case I was able to decide I couldn't help and not to feel
anxious or guilty about this decision.

A colleague in the summer program has offered another

illustration of a self-image. It is, I suspect, one that is more common to men than to women.

This friend was planning to take graduate work in American literature in the fall. He found himself deciding to use all his spare time during the summer in the Graduate Library of the University of California at Berkeley reading up on American literature. Suddenly he took stock of this decision. "Why," he thought, "do I feel it necessary to know all about a course before I take it? What sort of self-image is impelling me to act this way?"

In the first ten days of trying to become aware of when a self-image was working, what it was doing, what it was, how it affected other thoughts, emotions, actions, and my personality, I had recorded some hundred self-images that I could spot. Oddly enough, not one of these was related to my image as a female. One day Tarthang Rinpoche divided the group, with males sitting on one side of the room and females on the other. He instructed the women to tell the men what made them angry about the way men behaved. Afterwards the men were to tell the women what angered them about the way women behaved. . . . After this exercise I wrote down forty-nine negative self-images that had to do with my being born a girl. There were also seven positive ones. The negative ones began with, "Girls aren't good for men, therefore I'm not good for men." The positive ones began with, "I have a lot of attractive energy and warmth."

I had a certain amusement in looking over these forty-nine negative self-images, deciding they were useless, reclaiming the energy they imprisoned, and letting them fade away into nothing. It was a great relief to get that part of the attic (or the cellar) cleaned out.

Looking deeper

Shortly after this, Rinpoche stimulated the discovery of more self-images by giving us an exercise which brought us

New approaches, age-old teachings. A dialogue preceding a meditation session with Tarthang Tulku Rinpoche.

face to face with some of our early childhood emotional states, "density" states of wrath, frustration, and depression. This unearthed for me a self-image that was quite desperate about its fate. It began, "I won't be the girl!" and proceeded through, "I can't help being!" to, "I can't! I can't! I can't!" to, "I *can*— be sad." One can easily see how this progression of energy from such a passionately frustrated self-image could set the color and tone for a whole personality pattern and affect one's choice of coping mechanisms. It was good to get rid of that one and get back the energy from it.

Rinpoche warned us that when we thought we had the answers about our self-images, when we had learned what it was that lay behind a certain view of ourselves or certain actions we were taking, that these still probably weren't the right answers and that we should look more deeply.

He suggested that the real culprits did not show themselves that easily.

Often I had dreams that shed light on images that were puzzling and didn't want to come out during the day. I had a dream about the image who would *not* be the girl that led me to this clarification. I have a twin brother. Our mother died within days after delivery as a result of complications from the birth. Somewhere, somehow, I had gotten hold of the idea that if it hadn't been for the girl and the emergency measures that had to be taken with her delivery, Mother might have been saved. Therefore my not wanting to be *the* girl did not have as much to do with my thinking the status of women inferior as with my desperate desire to avoid being saddled with the responsibility of my mother's death. As you see, it was rather deep material we were getting into. But we were given tools to handle such situations, particularly the technique of "sitting with" strong emotions we wanted to observe during meditation.

A chance to observe results

Already I have had a chance to examine some differences in my behavior. There was an opportunity for a "pilot observation" of changes in operation when my husband Ron came for a weekend visit at the end of the sixth week of the program. It gave me some perspective on what had been happening inside me. It was like being able to estimate better how tan you have become during the summer by looking into a mirror in August if you haven't looked at one since June.

The whole weekend was, quite simply, fun. That was one of the differences. There was not a single instance when I wished Ron had behaved in a different way. That is a change in attitude. I can never remember our being together for three days before when I hadn't wished some little thing were different. I found myself behaving differently too. There was an incident when we had a difference of opinion about the street to take to get back to the hotel. Ron was about to take a street up the hill. I wasn't sure where it went. I *was* sure how to get back to the hotel. In the past I might have said, "You can't reach the hotel that way." To which he might easily have responded, "Who says I can't?" or "There's always fun in a challenge." This type of response has had the effect in the past of making me feel uninfluential, to say the least. This time I just said, "The hotel is on Ashby. Ashby is back here." Then I turned around and walked toward Ashby. So did Ron. Before this, I would have waited for him to move toward Ashby, and I would have felt frustrated if he hadn't.

There were also many other subtle differences in my responses to situations as they came up and in my taking initiative to make things happen. Here is an example of a difference in response which perhaps no one but I would ever notice, for it was an inward difference. I was talking on the phone to a friend who had given Ron a necklace to give to me. He indicated in pantomime that I shouldn't forget to mention the gift. Outwardly I probably behaved much as I would have before. But inwardly there was a great difference, and that difference gave the whole episode a different quality than it would have had previously. Before, I would have thought, "For crying out loud! Of course I'll mention the present. Why do you think I'm on the phone anyway? What kind of a dope do you take me for?" This time I had a moment's hesitation, a space in which I was conscious of letting awareness take over and habit fade out. Then I thought, "He's supporting me by reminding me to remember." Somehow, with no specific intention on my part to do it, I seem to have lost much of my defensiveness.

Here is just one further difference I would like to report. There was a time somewhere toward the end of our weekend together when I was tempted to ask Ron, "Do you notice any changes in me?" Six weeks before that I would probably have gone ahead with that impulse and asked the question.

But this time I had a change of mind. "Why ask?," I thought. "I know I'm different. If he hasn't noticed it doesn't matter. I don't need outer validation to make it a fact for me." After Ron left he wrote me a letter mentioning changes he had noticed, including some I had not been aware of.

I found that by attaching my self-esteem to certain self-images, I had been limiting my ability to appreciate. Getting rid of self-images, releasing their holding power, opened up the capacity for esteem, both for myself and for others.

Notes

1. Robert M. Pirsig, *Zen and the Art of Motorcycle Maintenance* (New York: Morrow, 1974), p. 280.

2. Tarthang Tulku, "The Self-Image," *Crystal Mirror* (1974) 3:33–34.

Ground of Enlightenment

James L. Gauer

Do we approach the question of enlightenment from the end or from the beginning? If we look towards the end, the path looms long and awesome. If we look at the beginning, one footstep doesn't seem so momentous, taxing, or frightening. Having a beginner's mind, I prefer to deal with the start. And the beginning is just as important as the ending. They may be one and the same.

We will deal here with a major ground of the way of

JAMES L. GAUER has a B.A. and Ph.L. degrees from St. Louis University and an M.Div. degree from the Jesuit School of Theology at Berkeley. Focusing on human development through creative self-expression, he has taught self-integration utilizing such art forms as drama, music, photography, television, and film, both in the United States and the Orient. At the time of this writing he was teaching at the Nyingma Institute and continuing his research in aesthetic perception and the psychology of creative consciousness at the Graduate Theological Union in Berkeley.

enlightenment—the practice of pure awareness. In Tibetan Buddhist terminology, it is called *shin jhong*. *Shin jhong* develops awareness. *Shin* means extreme, big, or highest. *Jhong* means finally, completely achieved, perfectly learned. So from the word itself we get the feel of awareness extremely perfected, complete to the highest degree.

Space

Sooner or later in the process of personal growth, we must face the question of space—our own psychological space, others' space, and shared space. We must ask ourselves questions like, "How large is my space? What occupies my space? Can others easily enter my space? And what happens when they do?"

Our urban environment and the proliferation of information intensify our feelings of physical and psychological crowding. Frequently we react to this cramping with an accusation, "You don't give me enough space." Or else we plead, "I need my own space." But do I want to empty my space out or fill it up, or both? How do I empty it or fill it?

Since we're facing the problem of crowding, we might begin by looking at emptying. If I want to create emptiness, I have at least two methods: first, I can remove the objects one by one which occupy my space. Or, I can place the objects in my space further apart so that I create emptiness between the objects. The first method works best in handling unwanted physical and emotional invaders. Through physical relaxation and massage, for example, we uproot kinks, knots, and bumps which claim ground in the physical organism and solidly obstruct the free flow of energy. By dissolving, pulling out, or unlocking these intruders, we open space in which we feel physically freer. We experience a comfortable and liberated physical place to be in the world, namely our own body. In a similar fashion, when we undo a severe emotional blockage, we experience ourselves as standing taller and straighter, feeling larger. When we therapeutically re-experience a suppressed childhood resentment against a parent, we enlarge our present awareness to encompass a felt past historical event. We have established a more unified and larger historical continuum of experience.

The second "space saving" method of placing objects further apart so that we experience the emptiness between them applies most readily to mind objects, or rather, thoughts. Many of us lead a mental life similar to the Los Angeles freeway at rush hour. On structures allegedly designed to provide maximum freedom and swiftness of movement, our thoughts honk along bumper to bumper in a polluted atmosphere. If a frustrated driver tries to look around, he discovers only other trapped drivers. Only rarely do we find ourselves in a position to discriminate lucidly what other kinds of drivers are moving in that stream. The more we strive to push our way through the jam, the more likely we are to collide. At this point a voice might suggest that if we put some distance between the vehicles, the journey might not be so frustrating. And if there were no vehicles there at all, we might actually experience a *free*-way. "But then aren't you devaluing the mind and deprecating thoughts?" comes the objection. And the reply, "No, I'm just suggesting that there might be another way to travel in the mind. Perhaps you should consider *space* travel. Have you ever thought that you could live in and experience the space between thoughts?" This challenges us immediately since it suggests that our naive equation of thoughts and mind is a confused one. We are asked here to get out of a routinized thought pattern and to experience a new aspect of mind. Perhaps our grasping for solid thoughts has only cluttered our minds and fenced off true experience. At the risk of belaboring an already comical analogy, I'd suggest that we might feel freer, have more space, and get where we want to go faster by flying above our muddle in something like the transparent bubble of a helicopter.

Transparency

In spite of its limitations, "transparency" at least begins to point at the experience even though it may mislead us into thinking that some "thing" actually exists through, *trans*, which we look. ("Suchness," "void," "emptiness" have been used to indicate this state of consciousness though each has its own shortcomings of overuse, fearsomeness, or vacuity.) Such transparency would be a barrier, a shield that protects us from something. Pure awareness of *shin jhong* doesn't protect in that sense because protection assumes that something or someone out there frightens us. We protect ourselves against fearful threats. To achieve transparency, we must already have controlled the fear which projects hostile antagonists outside ourselves. With no fear, we have no need for protection. We can expose ourselves directly to reality as it is. Transparency is not something that stands between us as subject and the perceived object.

Thoughts frequently mediate our experience for us. "Transparency," here, has no mediating characteristic. Without a medium, we experience directly, naturally, "transparently."

Silence

The state of awareness known as *shin jhong* requires one essential quality rare in our noisy heads—silence. Since many of us live in a noise-polluted environment, we don't experience the natural gifts which come from silence. Just as we don't feel our own empty space, so also we can't rest easily in our own silence. Full and total silence must permeate our body, our breath, our mind, and our speech before inner awareness of being can emerge. In such a silence we do not feel that we "have" breath, thoughts, and perceptions, nor are we watching them from an observer viewpoint. Rather, we just experience them, we are the experience.

Although a quiet, spacious setting facilitates the development of a meditative silence for ourselves, it is not absolutely necessary since we are speaking of inner silence. With sufficient practice we may be able to carry such tranquility into stressful situations and to transform many normally harrying stimuli into events enveloped by our mental calm.

We can recognize the advantages of such a state easily enough—a balanced disposition, a lessening of compulsive responses, the capacity to see a situation as it is without bias, a decrease of tension and nervousness, an increased mental agility, and more creative problem solving. The ability to remember clearly and a pervasive mental "playfulness" grow in this state as well. This practice can also influence other realms of our psyche in less familiar ways. Psychic phenomena such as clairvoyance, clairaudience, and clairsentience may occur in the *shin jhong* level of awareness.

Psychic phenomena

In many people's minds the notion of "psychic phenomena" triggers a good deal of mythology. Looking at psychic abilities from a more realistic viewpoint, we see that these capacities demand two qualities: receptivity and clarity. Being "open" or "in touch" come with the heightened state of awareness of *shin jhong*. Psychic receptivity seems to manifest a magnetic quality as if the psychic were drawing extrasensory perceptions to himself or herself. It is almost as if the silence characteristic of *shin jhong* is so dense, so complete that it forms a powerful magnetic "space" in which subtle vibrations not perceived by the five senses can be seen, heard, and felt.

The second condition is clarity. Sensitive psychic awareness precludes confusion. In order for the psychic to be genuinely clear about what is happening in another's mind, his or her own mind must be uncluttered by personal subjective mental vibrations; otherwise, messages will be tainted by

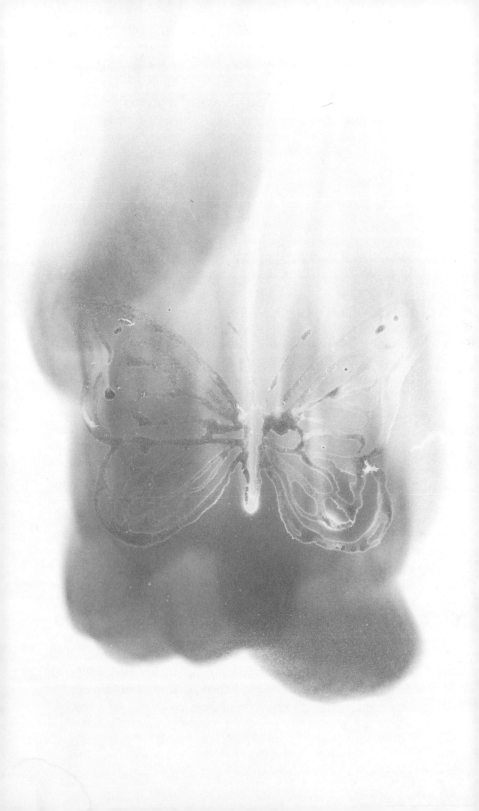

doubts, fears, or ignorance. Clearness characterizes the enhanced special quality of the mind in *shin jhong*. Hence the tradition speaks of "pure" or "pristine" awareness.

Memory

The information explosion, it is generally agreed, has over-taxed our memories. We store and recall surplus quantities of factual data for efficient functioning at work, and then find at times that the simplest everyday items evade our recollection. The first-rate heart surgeon wonders where he forgot his car keys. What causes us to blank out? It seems as if our high speed memory tapes shut down periodically to provide a moment's rest in an overprogrammed schedule. Memory, moreover, depends upon awareness. We don't remember what we weren't aware of because of distractedness. The sharper the awareness of an experience, the more vivid our memory of it will be.

Memory also fails us in a more profound way. We forget ourselves. We recede into mechanical or habitual reactions and then wonder, "Now, why did I do a thing like that?" or "I thought I had worked through that one." When we forget ourselves, we forget others, take them for granted, and our relationships suffer.

How does the *shin jhong* state relate to memory? It is said that with this awareness, in the space the size of one sesame seed, you can visualize the whole universe. Why not then visualize our entire lifetime within the space of our own body? The tradition says that a highly developed practitioner can visualize ten thousand Buddhas in a second or think ten thousand thoughts in a second. This certainly seems hyperbolic until we realize that with our eyes we can perceive a network of ten thousand pieces of colored glass as a beautiful mosaic. With absolute mental calm and highly attuned clarity perhaps we can visualize our life as an icon of gold pieces in which memories do not remain isolated events of a disconnected past but rather shine as integrated jewels in a becoming whole. The perfectly calm mind remains tranquil whether one, ten, or ten thousand events are present to it. We could perhaps accept particular experiences, then, not as a hazy conglomerate of isolated sensations, thoughts, and feelings, but as the free functioning of each of our processes within the continuum of our being.

Mental playfulness

A sharp memory relates closely to mental playfulness. Mental playfulness can be applied to the past, but here we will look at present and future mental events. One of our most rewarding and even sublime faculties accomplishes itself in generating new ideas. Sometimes great minds unravel the final knot of a new discovery or theory in a dream or in a vision, as in the case of Einstein. For most of us, unraveling more mundane problems with creative insight takes time and effort. One essential quality native to the flexible mind is the ability to wonder about questions and to play with possible answers.

In our daily lives as well, we search for new options, but usually, because of our fixations, we end up resorting to the old standbys deeply ingrained in us. This leads to a habituated, flat, one-dimensional approach to living and consequently to fatigue, boredom, discouragement, and depressed emotional states.

Meditative awareness, however, acts as a strong antidote to this downward spiral because it requires that we don't fixate on anything. Thoughts and feelings become loose, relaxed, unattached. Rather than becoming either passive or tight, we allow the pure source of energy which is our awareness to become available to us. Energy, enthusiasm, lightness, and clarity characterize this state. In this purified lightness, then, we can float any problem, idea, or emotion and play with it. We can look at these balloons freely floating in our empty space from all directions, not just from one side, since our awareness encompasses every direction relative to the suspended mind object. We can even laugh at ourselves as we struggle with difficulties, laugh in such a way that we actually resolve them. We can enjoy this playful agility because we aren't holding onto positions. Taking a position implies that "I," "me," or "ego" has fixated itself. And once we fixate ourselves, that inner dialogue starts which can continue day and night with its well-known cast of thousands. With the energy available through nonfixated awareness, however, we can make thoughts malleable. We can catch them, stretch them, curl them. We can even get inside of them or stay on the outside or do both simultaneously. We can reverse an idea and see where it started, or run it ahead and view its outcome. We can see thoughts in slow or fast motion. The *shin jhong* state allows us to pull things out of the darkness into the light of awareness and then to play by surrounding them with a myriad of rainbow colors. In such states it seems that pure awareness itself creates energy, an energy whose playfulness is indistinguishable from creativity and insight.

Growing up in Adulthood: Stages on the Buddhist Path

James Shultz

Much of Buddhist theory and practice is an applied developmental psychology facilitating growing up in adulthood.[1] Unlike much of Western developmental psychology, Buddhist psychology has focused on releasing the highest potential of adults. Adults who tap into the full human potential are exemplified in Buddhism by Bodhisattvas—those enlightened persons who assist others toward Enlightenment. Using Abraham Maslow's term, we might call them "meta-normal adults." Maslow, who coined the well-known terms "peak experience" and "self-actualization," ended his long career with

JAMES SCHULTZ has a Ph.D. in Human Development from the University of Chicago, and was a Program Director in Higher Education for the National Training Laboratories in Washington D.C. A consultant for several educational and religious institutions, he served as the Nyingma Institute's first vice-president, where he taught East/West therapy, introductions to Buddhist thought, and the nature and value of contemplation.

the study of adults whom he saw not only as self-actualizing, but whose lives also partook of the transcendent and the ultimate. Throughout his lifework, Maslow aimed at correcting what he contended was the over-emphasis by modern Western psychology on animal, child, and abnormal psychology to the neglect of normal and "meta-normal" adult functioning. In one of his last books entitled *The Farther Reaches of Human Nature*,[2] he presented the notion of "Being Value Leaders," adults who embody wholeness, goodness, aliveness, truth, richness, completion, playfulness, meaningfulness, simplicity, order, effortless energy, beauty, and dichotomy-transcendence. While maintaining an emphasis on rigorous empirical methodology, Maslow broke with the behaviorist assumption that only externally visible physical phenomena can be known, and utilized, as does Buddhism, a more phenomenological and existential method which focused on the human experience as it is from the inside, as known by the most alert and sensitive observers of the inner life.[3]

Erik Erikson, a psychoanalyst in the neo-Freudian tradition, revised and extended Sigmund Freud's scheme of infantile developmental stages by defining eight major cumulative life-stages, each containing an existential polarity: Trust vs. Mistrust (first year of life); Autonomy vs. Shame and Doubt (second year); Initiative vs. Guilt (ages 3–5); Industry vs. Inferiority (primary school years); Identity vs. Diffusion (adolescence); Intimacy vs. Isolation (young adulthood); Generativity vs. Stagnation (middle age); Integrity vs. Despair (old age).[4] Erikson's stage theory does not neglect growing up in adulthood as it places four of the eight important stages after childhood. His descriptions may be seen to parallel Buddhist ideas, as Generativity is similar to Compassion and Integrity is similar to Wisdom.

An important feature in Erikson's thought is that development of adults is viewed as a continuing expansion of the pliability and openness of the child. Adulthood need not be a time of fixed, narrow specialization if we keep alive flexibility, openness, and appreciative capacity. Continuing child-like openness into adulthood is also a theme in Buddhism. This can be misunderstood unless we realize that Buddhist practice assumes a foundation of mature life experience which is then to be placed in a larger perspective.

Erikson emphasized the importance of what he called a psycho-social "moratorium"—a time to wander and test out roles before settling down to commitments—in the development of adolescents and young adults. The moratorium could result in a richer and more genuine adult identity by avoiding premature foreclosure of options in regard to occupation, sexual and family roles, ideology, etc. In Buddhist cultures one traditionally entered the spiritual path only in late adulthood, after the stage of being a "householder" and raising a family. This could be considered a second "moratorium" in later life.

Like all paths for the development of "meta-normal" adults, Buddhist practice needs access to time and energy and requires some degree of withdrawal, that is, a moratorium from ordinary adult roles and preoccupations. Adults, like children, need space to grow in, not only physical but psychological space. The adult needs time to meditate and to consider broader human questions.

The Swiss psychologist, Jean Piaget, uncovered the importance of cognition in the overall pattern of human development. He showed cognition to be much wider and richer than what we ordinarily call intelligence.[5] Piaget has shown that the child thinks with and through bodily activity. Infantile sensory-motor cognition gradually develops into concrete thinking which only later emerges as adult language and logic. The child's model of reality is built up gradually as part of a holistic developmental process. Piaget, as does Buddhism, understood cognition, not simply as quantitative or verbal ability, but as a far-reaching, inclusive human potential which includes motivations, motor activities, perceptions of time and space, morality, and feelings. In Buddhism the analysis of cognition was combined with what could be seen as a therapeutic method for releasing the fullness of cognitive awareness.

The developmental psychologies of Piaget and Erikson each show six requisite characteristics of an effective stage theory. First, there are various cumulative levels, and with each level, there is preparation leading to higher levels. Second, the progression is viewed as being a relatively fixed sequence common to human beings, though few reach the higher stages. Third, a stage is a functional equilibrium, and the name for a stage is heuristic, not implying any specific, underlying physical structure corresponding directly to function. Fourth, the shift from one stage to another is a fundamental change in the functional equilibrium. Fifth, fixation (staying too long at a stage) or regression (trying to return to an earlier stage) blocks further development. Sixth, attempts to short-cut the process by jumping directly to the highest stage are usually not successful. These six characteristics seem also to be exemplified by the traditional Buddhist account of the stages on the Bodhisattva path.

Maslow's research, combined with the work of Piaget and Erikson, can serve to clarify the criteria for empirical verification of higher stages of development. First, a higher stage is not arbitrarily defined but has, empirically, the lower stages as its functional prerequisite. Usually only a small percentage of the population are in the higher stage of development, so we should not confuse what is average with what is the highest potential. Second, a higher stage is the preferred felt-experience for people who have experienced both options. Third, a higher stage is capable of assimilating more internal differentiation and a wider range of external phenomena. It shows a functional equilibrium which is both more stable and more open because it is adequate to assimilate more of reality. The Buddhist account of the stages on the Path has been subjected to empirical testing over many centuries and cultures, and can be said to satisfy these three criteria.

In what follows we draw upon Erikson, Piaget, and Maslow in proposing a tentative stage theory of adult spiritual development. Five stages are suggested. The literature of Buddhism includes many classic discussions of the stages of spiritual development. One of the best known is the Five Paths described by sGam-po-pa.[6] When the many Tibetan texts on the Five Paths (in Western terms, the five stages) are translated into English, they will offer a detailed map for spiritual travelers, describing in detail the various characteristics and the necessary conditions for spiritual progress into higher stages. In abbreviated form, the five stages are:

1. Preparatory (*tshogs-lam, sambhāramārga*). This assumes an adequate foundation in worldly knowledge, including ethics and manners.

2. Linkage to the goal (*sbyor-lam, prayogamārga*). Beginning to have the goal clearly in view.

3. Seeingness (*mthong-lam, darśanamārga*). A clearer view of the goal and the path. Absence of doubts. Working toward the goal. Recognition of the Four Noble Truths.

4. Concentrated Practice (*sgom-lam, bhāvanāmārga*). Staying within meditative awareness. The path now provides one with enough strength to cure oneself and to make progress on one's own momentum.

5. Fulfillment in Buddhahood (*mthar-phyin-pa'i-lam, nisthāmārga*).

While drawing inspiration from the traditional discussion of the Five Paths, the following presentation is not intended to parallel them exactly, although the highest stage will be understood as Buddhahood. The five stages, from the beginning to the fulfillment, indicate this progressive unfolding as increasingly inclusive, with higher stages building upon and transcending lower stages.

Stage I:
Beginning on the foundation of childhood precursors

Buddhism assumes that adult spiritual development will base itself on an adequate foundation in worldly knowledge, including logic, ethics, manners, and that it is also based on the experience of all the prior stages of emotional and cognitive development. When Buddhism appeals to nonverbal, open awareness, it is in addition, and as an antidote, to prior psychic structuralization. It is wrong to consider Buddhist meditation as anti-intellectual. It is meta- and post-intellectual. Mystical cognition is understood as including formal cognition in a larger context. (Those stages of development which are a precondition for the Path, we will refer to from here on as the "childhood precursors.")

As life experience accumulates, we become lost in a fragmented and narrow world of socially defined roles, opinions, biases, specializations, and bits and pieces of knowledge. We are compulsively led about by our self-image, which, in its narrowness, cuts us off from our liberating cognitive capacity. This self-image provides a false sense of uniqueness and freedom while simultaneously forcing us to function at a restricted level.

Aware persons begin to recognize, as experience accumulates, that a change needs to be made in their over-all organization of themselves; the childhood precursors provide an inadequate functional equilibrium in the sense that they are unable to assimilate the full range and richness of inner and outer experience. Just as arithmetic, though a useful foundation, points beyond itself to higher mathematics, what we have attained in childhood points beyond to a higher stage of truth and appreciation.

Stage II:
Peak experiences and aspiration for Enlightenment

The second stage emerges when the functional equilibrium built around formal cognition, social roles, and other "childhood precursors" gives way to a more inclusive equilibrium built around peak experiences and the aspiration for Enlightenment.

The Buddhist path becomes formulated in this stage as a clear personal goal, beginning when mystical and peak experiences break through the narrow self-image, and culminates when we have a strong, clear aspiration for Enlightenment. This stage is a process of interiorizing ourselves through intense experiences such as peace, insight, relaxation, beauty, ecstasy, confidence, friendship, grief, meaningfulness. While sexual and drug-related experiences could and do serve as peak experiences, Buddhism has largely viewed these with skepticism because they tend to create a dependency or even an addiction to an external physical stimulus and, in searching for such obvious physical experience, we may have difficulty appreciating the more subtle but ultimately more satisfying meditative states. Such states may be highly conscious, aware moments closely connected with confidence and insight, where we observe ourselves both sensitively and integratively, breathe more deeply, and feel a sense of oneness in all directions. Meditation does not fixate or addict us but refines itself naturally from momentary excitements toward more lasting bliss, from erotic feelings toward empathy, from emotionality toward understanding, from dependency toward self-sufficient strength and generosity. Meditation in a Buddhist context is not just an isolated technique but an organic developmental process.

The aspiration for Enlightenment may be seen as what Maslow calls a plateau experience, being a continuing, overriding desire for a pervasive extension of the qualities felt in peak moments into all of our life-space and life-time. Peak experiences, by definition, are ephemeral, while a plateau experience, though just as alive, is more stable. The aspiration for Enlightenment, as a plateau experience, includes confidence and relaxation. It is not an anxious striving toward some far-off goal. The process of being on the Path is intrinsically rewarding at each stage.

Stage III:
Community, compassion and strength

The third stage emerges when one graduates from being primarily interested in the quest for a wide variety of peak experiences and decides to join a specific Buddhist spiritual community, and to follow a specific Buddhist teacher in the learning of compassion and strength. Buddhist teachings emphasize the need for adequate experience and thought before commiting oneself to the Path and to membership in the Sangha, the community of those on the Path. These prerequisites are meant to protect the Buddhist practitioner from the overconformity and fanaticism more characteristic of prose-lytizing groups who seek rapid conformity to the community. Full membership in the Sangha comes when the aspiration for enlightenment has stabilized.

At this stage we are no longer shopping around in the psycho-spiritual growth marketplace nor seeking to invent our own unique, eclectic spiritual or psychological path. We are relatively clear about the truth of the Buddha's teaching and are ready wholeheartedly to concentrate our energies on mastering the fundamentals of its spiritual discipline.

According to the teachings of Buddhism, the six great strengths to be developed, the *pāramitās*, are generosity, morality, patience, vigor, meditative awareness, and wisdom. These "six perfections" increasingly replace our weakness, confusion, impulsiveness, and selfishness with more universal cognitive qualities capable of assimilating a vast range of inner and outer experience. As members of the Sangha our practice of the six perfections is tested in daily interaction with others who are on the Path and who share some consensus as to what the practice entails. Tasks that the outsider may see as mere discipline are, in the Buddhist tradition, also part of a growth process in which each person's varied capacities are fostered by the community.

Stage III necessarily comes after Stage II because peak

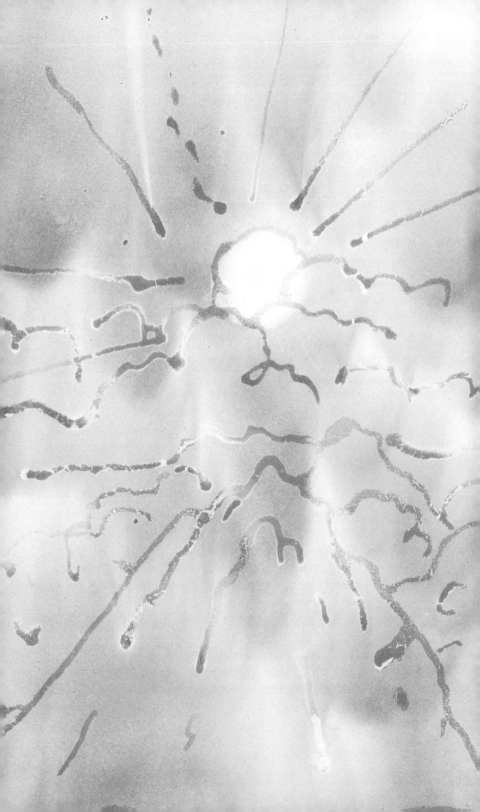

experiences and aspiration are needed to provide a motivating spirit which will infuse the learning of community, compassion, and strength. This stage necessarily precedes Stage IV because community, compassion, and strength are a necessary protection as we enter the ocean-like psychological and spiritual depths of the next stage. Only when we have learned to have compassion for and take care of ourselves and others can we trust ourselves to travel safely in the deepest psychological exercises of Buddhism.

Stage IV:
Deep psychological awareness and spirituality as Tantra

Stage IV begins when again, as in Stage II, our focus turns inward, this time not to seek gratifying peak experiences but to seek only the raw truth, be it pleasant or painful, at the foundation of our minds. In this stage we fully integrate Buddhist philosophy with our personal experience. Here our progress in the Dharma takes on a momentum of its own, and our spiritual development becomes a self-unfolding process. Further learning now takes place not so much by conscious effort but in the way a fire, once started, spreads naturally.

Buddhism teaches that a key aspect of deepening psychological awareness is learning to see the phenomenal world as apparition, or as a "dream." This Buddhist concept of apparition can be misunderstood as a denial of the relative constancy and independence of objects. The truth of apparitionalness in no way denies empirical regularities subject, for example, to scientific observation. Piaget has described in detail how the child increasingly recognizes patterns. The child sees stabilities and repetitions in encounters with his world and observes increasingly complex causal interrelationships and learns indirect methods of problem solving. He sees farther, and in larger pictures. He is able to foresee long-term future results. To realize all phenomena as apparitional in the Buddhist sense is not some regression to naive unawareness. It is meant rather to keep formal cognition from hypertrophying and reifying itself. It is to realize, in the ultimate sense, that phenomena are perceived and that our accurate, meaningful perceptions and responses depend on keeping alive the intrinsic awareness which enabled us to perceive regularities and patterning in the first place. If we neglect our intrinsic awareness, we lose our wholeness as persons and our ability to continue seeing reality as it is. We forget that all so-called phenomena are, psychologically speaking, perceptions of *relative* concreteness and permanence. We need not confuse our labels for phenomena with the phenomena themselves or with the fullness of our own cognitive Being. The loss of intrinsic awareness is the first link (*ma-rig-pa*, *avidyā*—traditionally translated as ignorance) in the Twelvefold Chain of Causation.[7] This loss of intrinsic awareness lets us fall into a craving nature which separates and attaches, producing the suffering inherent in the various manifestations of samsaric existence.

In Stage IV the practitioner relates the literature of Buddhist psychology to his own experience. Traditionally, he will learn to recognize experientially the fifty-one mental function-events described in the Buddhist Abhidharma.[8] He will begin to understand how his mental state at any point in time is some combination of these various function-events. He learns to recognize how fear, doubt, confusion, and other emotional states can operate as controlling forces in our lives.

It is said that the fifty-one mental events of the Abhidharma were originally written down as brief meditation lists, handed from one practitioner to another like a road map, meant to indicate, in effect, "When this happens, watch for this. The six major negative emotions you will encounter in your practice are these. . . ." Buddhist psychology is essentially oriented toward assisting practitioners in the process of deepening their awareness through meditation.

Beyond the Abhidharma, which is shared by all Buddhists,

Nyingma psychology is unique in emphasizing the importance of contact with nine major types of consciousness, especially the two deepest, most homogeneous types, *kun-gzhi*
and *kun-gzhi rnam-shes*, which lie below the five sensory cognitions (seeing, hearing, smelling, tasting, and touching),
mentation, and self-image. *Kun-gzhi*, the deepest, accounts
for the continuity and homogenity of mind.

The experience of contacting *kun-gzhi* arises out of meditation under the guidance of a teacher. This contact can be a
deeply therapeutic process. As one contacts *kun-gzhi* and
makes it less dark and heavy, a sense of lightness and apparitionalness pervades cognition. Though comparable to the
Western idea of the subconscious in terms of depth, *kun-gzhi*
is knowable and transformable. It is an experience beyond
words, an experience of relatively pure cognitive energy as a
wide open field of potentiality. *Kun-gzhi* is viewed by the Nyingma as the all-ground, from which all specific aspects emerge
as subdivisions and distinct cognitive events in the ordinary
mind. Contact with *kun-gzhi* is deeply peaceful and unifying
since it is the mind's contact with its own homogeneity and
continuity.[9]

Although contact with *kun-gzhi* is satisfying and positive,
Nyingma psychology counsels us of the dangers of becoming
stuck in *kun-gzhi* since such contact is not the ultimate in
spiritual development. Many practitioners, tradition relates,
have made the mistake of stopping at *kun-gzhi*, but the enlightened practitioner has gone "beyond" *kun-gzhi* to *ye-shes*
which is actual, absolute, total knowingness.

The latter part of Stage IV introduces a spirituality beyond
mere psychology. It is not only self-understanding, but understanding in its broadest sense. *Ye-shes* includes the capacity to
discern the ultimate and live with conviction within the felt
presence of the ultimate. Unlike Western cultures, Tibetan
Buddhism did not develop a split between secular psychology
and religious experience. In Tantric Buddhism, analytical

psychology merges into the development of worship and spiritual awareness. This spirituality is honest, alive, and enriched because it unfolds on the foundation of psychological awareness. It is because of this that the well-developed forms of worship in Tantric Buddhism are quite different from mere religiosity or pietism. This spirituality is a pure, non-dogmatic experiencing which does not reify the objects and symbols of worship.[10] In its fullest expression, spirituality is a conviction which combines openness and a full use of one's cognitive capacities with assurance, certainty, and peace.

Preparation for death is an important part of this spirituality, but this is accomplished without speculations about the continuation of an individual soul. In spirituality as Tantra, we learn to accept fully the transiency and insubstantiality of all phenomena including ourselves, and this becomes the basis for joy and freedom. Longchenpa, in his work *The Natural Freedom of Mind,* wrote:

> Since Mind-as-such—pure from the beginning and with no root to hold to something other than itself—has nothing to do with an agent or something to be done, one's mind may well be happy. . . . Since everything is but an apparition, perfect in being what it is, having nothing to do with good or bad, acceptance or rejection, one may well burst out in laughter.[11]

Stage V:
Buddhahood as union with the lineage of original Buddhist teachers

Those in this stage join the living lineage of Bodhisattvas who have become the fulfillment of the Buddhist Path and of human potentiality. The qualities of such exemplars show a high overlap with the "Being Values" described by Maslow, especially aliveness, wholeness, generosity, beauty, effortless energy, and dichotomy-transcendence. In Maslow's language, they transcend the false dichotomies of freedom and spontaneity vs. order, appropriateness, and discipline; mysticism vs. practical affairs and social organization; meditation vs. philosophical analysis; art vs. science. They also exhibit Erikson's "Generativity" and "Integrity" in compassionate action and spiritual wisdom. Instead of giving answers, they invite others to walk the path for themselves. Śākyamuni said:

> Although I showed you the means of liberation,
> You must know that it depends on you alone.[12]

Through their teaching and their presence they pass on to others the blessing of the lineage of original Buddhist teachers. The inner *maṇḍala* by which they live their lives is unusually universal and timeless, and includes all sentient beings past, present, and future.

Whatever our stage on the Path, it is in direct contact with this embodied spiritual lineage which provides us with the fullest vision of the potentiality for growing up in adulthood which is the revealed actuality of Buddha Nature in all of us.

This outline of the five stages is tentative. A more sophisticated theory might be developed and verified for a Western setting, drawing in a more scholarly fashion upon the extensive Buddhist literature about stages on the Path. An accurate view of stages might help discourage unnecessary fixation at lower stages or self-deception about being in a higher stage.

The purpose of the Path is to make the Buddhist teaching of the oneness of all reality an experiential fact. Most of us find ourselves living with relative truth. Pretending that "all is Buddha" is of little help when our mind is still functioning so as to produce fragmentation and confusion. We can best develop when we make increasing contact with reality by dealing with what is operational in us and then refine and transcend it. It is in this context that we benefit from the skillful means and the knowledge of the stages of the Path available to us in Buddhism.

Notes

1. This article is an outgrowth of personal experiences over several years of study of Buddhism. The idea of writing about stages on the Path emerged as I reread an earlier article I had written, "Early Experiences at Padma Ling," *Crystal Mirror* (1972) 2:74–79, and realized the extent to which my early contact with Buddhism was part of the stage of being dominated by the search for peak experiences. This led me to the notion of using Maslow, Erikson, and Piaget to reinterpret the stages of the Path. Spiritual development can be facilitated by being fully in our present stage and by knowing when we are ready to move into another stage. Realizing this, we begin to understand why stages of the Path received major emphasis in Buddhist literature.

2. Abraham H. Maslow, *The Farther Reaches of Human Nature* (New York: Viking, 1971).

3. See also Abraham H. Maslow, *Motivation and Personality*, 2nd ed. (New York: Harper & Row, 1970); *Religions, Values and Peak Experiences* (New York: Viking, 1970); *Toward a Psychology of Being* (New York: Van Nostrand, 1968).

4. See Erik Erikson, *Childhood and Society* (New York: Norton, 1964); *Gandhi's Truth* (New York: Norton, 1969); *Insight and Responsibility* (New York: Norton, 1964); *Young Man Luther* (New York: Norton, 1958).

5. See Jean Piaget, *The Construction of Reality in the Child* (New York: Basic Books, 1954); *The Language and Thought of the Child* (London: Routledge & Kegan Paul, 1952); *Logic and Psychology* (New York: Basic Books, 1957); *Judgment and Reasoning in the Child* (Totowa, N.J.: Littlefield, Adams, 1972); *The Moral Judgment of the Child* (Glencoe, Ill.: Free Press, 1948); *Origins of Intelligence in Children* (New York: Norton, 1963); *Psychology and Epistemology* (New York: Viking, 1971).

6. sGam.po.pa, *The Jewel Ornament of Liberation*, trans. Herbert V. Guenther (Berkeley: Shambhala, 1971), pp. 232–38.

7. Steven D. Goodman, "Situational Patterning: Pratītyasamut-pāda," *Crystal Mirror* (1974) 3:93–101.

8. Ye-shes rGyal-mtshan, *Mind in Buddhist Psychology*, trans. Herbert V. Guenther and Leslie S. Kawamura (Berkeley: Dharma Publishing, 1975).

9. Lawrence Gruber, "Kun-gzhi: The Positiveness of Being," *Crystal Mirror* (1974) 3:102–08. For a detailed reference defining the nine types of consciousness, see Herbert V. Guenther, *Buddhist Philosophy in Theory and Practice* (Baltimore: Penguin, 1972), pp. 109, 221.

10. The theory and practice of spirituality in Tantric Buddhism is described in detail by Herbert V. Guenther in the latter section of *Buddhist Philosophy in Theory and Practice*.

11. Long-chen-pa, "The Natural Freedom of Mind," trans. Herbert V. Guenther, *Crystal Mirror* (1975) 4.

12. Śākyamuni, "The Life Story of Śākyamuni Buddha," *Crystal Mirror* (1974) 3:21.

Criss-crossing the Christian-Buddhist Bridge

Tilden H. Edwards, Jr.

There are many different "bridges" from which one could relate the realm of Christianity to that of Buddhism. We could start from the history of religions and use that discipline's categories of development. Or we could compare the two traditions' theological and philosophical statements about reality. From an anthropological standpoint we would focus on the culturally functional aspects of each tradition. From a psychological one, we would focus on the ways each tradition views and deals with the mind. If our starting point

TILDEN H. EDWARDS, JR. is an ordained priest in the Episcopal Church. He holds a Ph.D. from Harvard University and a S.T.B. from Harvard Divinity School. He has served as Executive Director of the Metropolitan Ecumenical Training Center in Washington, D.C. He has also been an educational services consultant for a wide range of congregations, religious jurisdictions, seminaries, and other religious and secular organizations.

were a concern with ethics, we would focus on ethical teachings and the impact of each tradition on personal morality and social-political structure. And from the vantage point of art, we could see how the intuitions of the traditions were expressed in sacred music or images, in the poetry, dance, and theater of ritual.

However, as I am neither a scholar nor an artist, but rather an Episcopal priest, I would like to write from still another bridge, an existential one where I will view the territory from the vantage point of my personal experiences in contact with each tradition and my personal sense of value. This bridge seems appropriate since one understanding of a Christian priestly vocation is that of a personal "bridge person," who subjectively helps to link reality in its various aspects in ways that tap a deeper existential vision. Let me share, then, some of my experiences, my hunches, and my questions. And, as I am starting from my own experience, I should explain that the form of Buddhism I have had contact with is that of the Nyingma tradition of Tibet as it was presented by Lama Tarthang Tulku during the first Nyingma Institute summer program in 1973.

My special readiness for that experience at that point in my life, together with the teaching of Tarthang Tulku Rinpoche, led me to a still-emerging fresh way of "seeing" reality.

The "marks" of this awakening "sight" include the following:

1. A fresh awareness of the distinction between "being in reality as it is," and the various interpretations of it made by the screens of thought, feeling, and image.

2. A far deeper awareness of the human capacity to identify more and more acutely and to subtly live in the "still point" where reality is revealed as it is in its diversity, its unity, its emptiness and form, its relationality, and its ultimate descriptionlessness: the reality that is revealed when our chain of desires and fears cease. Related to this, I have a new clarity

about the priority of attentiveness to my own mind, rather than to books and analytical interpretations (at the same time affirming the real value of reading—especially works of experientially "enlightened" persons—in order to provide helpful guidelines for my developing experience).

3. An awareness of the "giveness" of this realization when it comes, beyond our efforts, beyond our controlled conceptions of self.

4. A clearer sense of the spontaneous, integral relation of this "awakening" to compassion: to a detached, "light," yet serious caring for life, and a sense of its ultimate affirmativeness.

5. A fresh view of the meaning of "lineage" and the formation of a "teacher-priest."

6. A sense of the intimate, integral relation of body, intellect, feelings, and imagination, and of the fluidity and ultimate interdependence between self and other, between this and that.

7. A fresh perspective on moral and liturgical practice and philosophy as part of what Tibetan Buddhism calls the "skillful means" toward wisdom and compassion.

Each of these insights has led me to a corollary insight into Christian faith. Paradoxical as it may seem, each insight has had a way of illuminating and deepening my Christian faith and understanding far more than it has confused or conflicted with it. Let me share these correlations.

• *The distinction between reality and our various interpretations of it* has led me to focus more and more on the *experience*, the *awareness*, behind the words of Jesus, and of others in the Christian tradition. The more my own meditation deepens, the more I sense the reality pointed to (but not captured by) such New Testament phrases as these: "The Kingdom of God is in the midst of you"; "I am in the world . . . but not of it"; "Whoever would save his life will lose it, and whoever loses his life for my sake will find it"; "Not I, but Christ lives in me"; "Whoever humbles himself

like this child, he is the greatest in the Kingdom of Heaven";
"He emptied Himself, taking the form of a servant"; "Do not
be conformed to this world but be transformed by the renew-
al of your mind."

• *The Nyingma emphasis on first-hand attention to the mind
and its experience* led me to focus more attention on its closest
parallels found in the Christian contemplative tradition. Following my Nyingma experience that summer, I spent a week
in a silent Ignatian (Jesuit) retreat where I had time to read
selectively from some of the great Christian mystics, such as
John of the Cross, Teresa of Avila, Ruysbroeck, the anony-
mous author of the *Cloud of Unknowing*, Eckhart, and certain
of the early Fathers. I was struck many times by the similarity
of their descriptions of their "enlightened" awareness to those
of Tarthang Rinpoche's and certain Buddhist texts. The cul-
tural/linguistic context, of course, leads at times to very
different symbolism. Perhaps the differences in symbols represent a more substantive difference, but I feel clear that
the *experience* behind differing interpretations is essentially
the same, and sometimes even the words are identical. Of
course, none of us can be certain whether such Christian-
inspired awareness is equivalent to the final Dharmakāya
description found in the Nyingma Buddhist lineage.

The constant "attentiveness" and many forms of moral-
ascetic practice cultivated by the Nyingmapa tradition I find
parallel to the constant "recollectedness" and moral-ascetic
practices cultivated in various higher Christian disciplines.
However, I do not think there is any parallel for the acute,
subtle awareness of very specific and different mind states
encountered enroute to enlightenment—to being "in God"
(i.e. *kun-gzhi*; *kun-gzhi rnam-shes, nyon-yid*, etc.). Here the
Nyingma tradition in particular, I believe, has a unique contribution to make to the Western religious community. What
Christians (and perhaps some other Buddhist sects) seem to
find more by accident and fumbling in the dark, I sense the
Nyingma tradition finds through a more clearly and consis-

tently mapped, careful, long-term, tested, and subtle route. (Of course, "being found" ultimately is beyond the controlled technique of either tradition. I am speaking here of ways of "clearing the way" for that transforming awareness.)

A contemporary Christian theologian, Dr. Donald Dawe, in a recent lecture stated that the very heart of the Christian Gospel affirms the "human potential" fulfilled in Jesus Christ's life, death, and resurrection as the "first fruits" of the Kingdom, a potential available to us all. He specifically cited his own recent experience with a group of refugee Tibetan lamas in India and Nepal as a welcome opportunity for him and other Christians to learn more of the human potential as this has been realized in the Tibetan Buddhist tradition. I affirm this theological context as a Christian, and I believe we have an enormous amount to learn from the careful "experiential lineages" of Tibet.

Other notable Christians in recent decades have cited the great value of certain Buddhist "developmental methodologies" to help Christians to plow their ground for the "enlightened," or "saving," or "liberating" awareness that lies behind the great symbols of the Christian faith.[1] My belief is that the Western Church at this point in its history is particularly weak in the conscious provision of careful, on-going, personally transmitted developmental paths for full spiritual development.

• My sense of the *"giveness" of deeper awareness in meditation*, as opposed to a sense of its coming through my own efforts, I find experientially parallel to my understanding of the subtle balancing between "grace" and "free will" in the long Christian theological dialogue about these. It is clear that our efforts in the form of patience, energy, attention, etc., are necessary in most cases to on-going development. It is just as clear that finally it is in the "letting go" of our efforts and controls and self-images that real development happens. It is our work and yet it finally is not our work: grace and its transformation happen when they happen, not precisely when we will them, and they provide what we could not know otherwise. Our efforts help us to recognize and incorporate what comes, but they do not of themselves give the ultimate realization. In the ultimate awareness the very concept of an ultimately separate self dissolves, and all is grace.

I am aware that the term "grace" and its connotation of a free gift could have no direct parallel in Tibetan Buddhist interpretation. However, I would maintain that it does help to denote a realization which is ultimately similar to the Buddhist one.

• *That "enlightened" awareness integrally involves compassionate caring for all sentient beings* identifies Mahāyāna Buddhist and Christian experience and aims very closely. I believe that such spontaneous compassion is more explicitly and perhaps differently seen in the Christian tradition as an indicator of the *ultimate value, "goodness," and trustworthiness of life* in its deepest heart, a value that leads Christians to name this heart as the Holy One, the Living God, who reveals Himself in and through all life. I am aware that "pastorally" the Mādhyamika tradition through Nāgārjuna (as one Buddhist example) spurns any designation for the ultimate, lest it be turned into something to grasp after and thus become an obstacle to that spiritual transformation which can come only through surrender of all images, of all places to "go."

The "Godhead" is viewed similarly in Christian tradition; however, there is less shying away from the use of divine imagery (in word and visible form) as a *means of approach* to the imageless one. The danger of becoming fixated on the images is great; yet, their potential usefulness as "skillful means" toward both awareness and compassion has been considered worth the risk for most Christian groups. Perhaps the Tibetan Buddhist tradition of thanka painting exemplifies the risk-taking that Buddhists sometimes undergo with imagery. When such pictorial imagery is undertaken, both traditions seem to take pains to safeguard them from mis-use in various ways.

Buddhist traditions appear to put much less energy into translating their awareness and compassion into an analysis

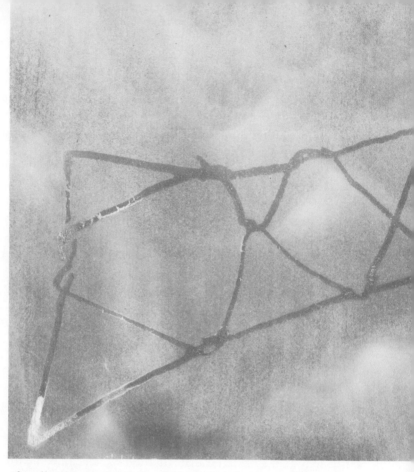

and collective activation of norms and means of justice in social-political structures, including those of the religious community itself. In most of the Christian tradition the "world" is seen as a "fallen realm" in a way at least obliquely parallel to the Buddhist understanding of samsara. Nonetheless, even though orthodox Christian theology and experience denies that "the Kingdom" can be brought in through any human social-political means, it still has struggled to express a compassion through attention to ameliorating societal oppressiveness in very energetic and on-going ways. Symbolic of this is the fact that "social ethics" is a category of learning in most Christian seminaries.

Related to this issue of societal compassion is the heav-

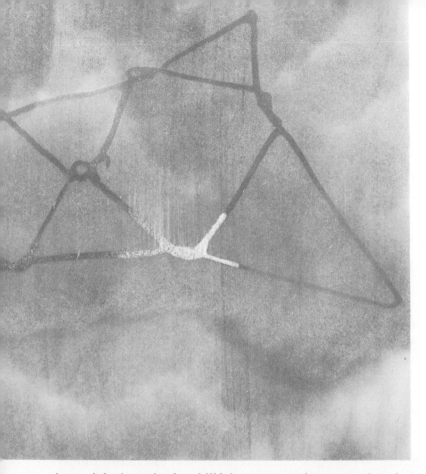

ier weight in attitude, skillful means, and energy placed on detailed forms of mutual caring and encouragement in the local Christian community than seems apparent in normal Buddhist versions of Sangha. I believe in this area that the Christian tradition has something to offer (even as Tibetan Buddhists can help Christians realize more fully the importance of time spent on experiential development of wisdom that when realized can lead to more *insightful* compassion).[2]

This potential Christian contribution to Buddhism, focused on social and communal analysis and concern, might be particularly valuable in the light of the contemporary situation in America and many other societies as interpreted by an American Buddhist in Japan, Gary Snyder:

The traditional Buddhist approach has been to get along with the morals of your society insofar as they don't run too counter to the Dharma and set up a new practice. But that's assuming a culture that knows what its own values are. There is nothing in the history of Buddhism to prepare you for the contingency of a society that doesn't have any clear values of its own, which leaves the field wide open.[3]

The importance of attention to this area is made more urgent by the incredibly fragile structural and environmental interdependence human societies now are in, and in the face of the increasingly threatening scarcity of energy, food, and land resources and of constructive opportunities for industrial expansion that probably will require a significant simplification of Western life styles and material expectations (just as meditation practices, of course, may aid such simplification). I do not think the struggle to translate our teachings in relation to this larger social context can be responsibly ignored today.

• The meaning of *lineage* and its carrier "teacher priests" in the Tibetan tradition, marked by a careful, long-term experiential passing on of the enlightenment process from teacher to "chela," opened my eyes to a clear weakness in Christianity at this point. "Apostolic succession" in consecration, ordination, baptism, and confirmation, the Christian equivalents of initiation into the "lineage," has been "passed on" primarily through a cognitive development and ritual process with only nominal attention to experiential development. Where "mind awareness" is focused upon, it tends to be either through an ecstatic "receiving of the Spirit" which is not usually developed critically beyond an initial experience and interpretation, or else it is focused upon through "clinical training" that borrows primarily from the inadequate framework of Western contemporary psychologies.

In certain contemplative Christian religious orders, such as Carthusians, Cistercians, and Carmelites, there seem to be the closest equivalents to "lineage" in its Tibetan meaning, but even here I sense that progress is expected more by stumbling than by being carefully, subtly led. Some Christians might rightfully retort that their focus is more on developing a direct relation to God accessible through Scripture and conscience than to any human mediary. Yet ordinarily it is through the wise mediary that tested, effective means of attentiveness to God may be learned.

• The *dynamic mind-body-feelings-imagination-world "integrality"* apparent in the Tibetan Vajrayāna tradition is a useful corrective to overcompartmentalization of different arenas of life so rife in Christianity (and even more so in Western science). This interdependence has been seen and practically approached in the Christian tradition at various times and in various ways, yet never (or very rarely), I sense, with the fullness of "skillful means" cultivated through the Nyingma lineage. In my own daily discipline and in my teaching of others, I have found Nyingma methods a very practical help.

• *Moral and liturgical practice and doctrinal statements* in Christian tradition too often have been seen as ends in themselves which the devout can attach themselves to rather than as means to deeper spiritual development. Nonetheless, there is consistent witness in the Christian tradition to the necessity of long "purgation" before one is free enough of ego-centeredness to move into the higher stages of "illumination" and "union" (to use the classic Christian ascetical terms). Both moral acts and liturgical rites can be means of purgation. Doctrinal statements (and their philosophical-theological base) can be seen as guides for developing experience, helping you to stay out of ruts along the way. In this ascetic context, all of these take on less of a legalistic and more of a "training ground" intentionality. This isn't necessarily their only intention, but I believe it is the most neglected one in contemporary Christian understanding.

In another sense, these practices and statements can legitimately be seen as ends in themselves and not just means. The

higher one's development, the more compassion spontaneously flows (though it may not be in culturally conventional
forms). The more "being present in God" (or awareness in
Reality as it is)—the realized heart of worship—is "sufficient,"
then the more interpretive, analogical words spontaneously
flow from the source of awareness, rather than from artifice.
Let me conclude with some open-ended questions about
possible existential commonalities in Christianity and Buddhism. To what extent are the following terms experientially
equivalent to one another?

1. Kingdom of God, Heaven and *Śūnyatā*.
2. Forgiveness of sins and liberation from *Karma* and
   Nirvāṇa.
3. Original Sin and *Avidyā* (primal ignorance).
4. *Agápe* (disinterested loving) and *Karuṇā* (compassion).
5. Being "beyond the Law" in Christ, and being beyond the
   dualism of good and evil.
6. "External" and "internal" revelation.
7. Triune God and the three-fold *Kāyas* (Bodies of the
   Buddha).
8. Unity of the divine and human in Christ and the non-
   dualistic nature of Reality.
9. Sin and *Kleśa* (obstruction).
10. Repentance and awareness of no ultimate self.
11. "This world" (fallen) and *saṃsāra*.
12. Gospel and *Dharma* (the teaching).
13. *Eklesīa* (community) and *Saṅgha* (community).
14. Jesus and Śākyamuni.
15. Invisible Church and esoteric tradition.
16. Angels, "powers and principalities" and peaceful and wrath-
    ful deities.
17. Iconoclasm (the First Commandment) and the "emptying of
    attachments" process.
18. Soteriological ("saving," "ultimately transforming") inten-
    tion and enlightenment intention.
19. The "Light which enlightens Everyman," "Logos" (Word),
    "Pneuma" (Spirit) and *Prajñā* (Wisdom).

The contemporary Roman Catholic theologian, John Dunne, has written:

> When one is no longer concerned about reaching agreement and restoring confidence in one's own culture, life, and religion, but simply about attaining insight and understanding, then one can enter freely into other cultures, lives, and religions and come back to understand one's own in a new light.[4]

May such an attitude pervade the future meetings of these traditions, on both sides, lest we miss out on the living water that only the empty cup can hold.

I am not personally very concerned about the boundaries between these two old, complex, many-faceted traditions, if indeed they exist at all at their esoteric heart, in the realized moments of both. I am most concerned about what we can learn from and share with each other, and what we can commonly witness in our current societal situation. The great recent Christian contemplative, Thomas Merton, has penetratingly stated the need for this common focus:

> The point to be stressed is the importance of serious communication, and indeed of "communion," among contemplatives of different traditions, disciplines, and religions. This can contribute much to the development of man at this crucial point of his history. Indeed, we find ourselves in a crisis, a moment of crucial choice. We are in grave danger of losing a spiritual heritage that has been painfully accumulated by thousands of generations of saints and contemplatives. It is the peculiar office of the monk in the modern world to keep alive the contemplative experience and to keep the way open for modern technological man to recover the integrity of his own inner depths.
>
> Above all, it is important that this element of depth and integrity—this element of inner transcendent freedom—be kept intact as we grow toward the full maturity of universal man. We are witnessing the growth of a truly universal consciousness in the modern world. This universal consciousness may be a consciousness of transcendent freedom and vision, or it may simply be a vast blur of mechanized triviality and ethical cliché.[5]

Notes

1. In regard to Tibetan Buddhism in particular, see Thomas Merton, *The Asian Journal* (New York: New Directions, 1973). In regard to Zen and Ch'an, see Thomas Merton, *Mystics and Zen Masters* (New York: Dell, 1969). In regard to Japanese Buddhist groups, see Dom Aelred Graham, *Conversations: Christian and Buddhist* (New York: Harcourt, Brace & Jovanovich, 1970); *Zen Catholicism: A Suggestion* (New York: Harcourt, Brace & Jovanovich, 1965). See also William Johnston, *The Still Point* (New York: Harper & Row, 1971); H. M. Enomiya-Lassalle, *Zen Meditations for Christians*, trans. John C. Maraldo (Lasalle, Ill.: Open Court, 1974). In regard to a wide range of Buddhist and Hindu traditions, see the wealth of valuable articles in *Cisterican Studies* (1974) 9, no. 2–3.

2. I am aware that there is a significant fresh social concern among many Buddhists, partly based on inherent Buddhist precepts and partly stimulated by Christian missionary example and secular social reform. See Yves Raguin, "How Buddhism Faces the Challenge of the Modern World," *Cistercian Studies* (1974) 9:277–96.

3. Dom Aelred Graham, *Conversations: Christian and Buddhist*, p. 81.

4. John Dunne, *The Way of All the Earth: Experiments in Truth and Religion* (New York: Macmillan, 1972), p. 44.

5. Thomas Merton, *The Asian Journal*, p. 317.

Index

THE NYINGMA PSYCHOLOGY SERIES
Books by Tarthang Tulku

Gesture of Balance, a guide to self-healing, awareness, and meditation. A heart-warming approach to attitudes and techniques that support inner honesty, confidence, growth, and change.

Openness Mind. How to work with negative feelings and deepen experience through meditation, visualization, and insight into the nature of mind.

Kum Nye Relaxation, Parts 1 and 2, A gentle self-teaching approach to physical, emotional, and spiritual fitness. Over 200 exercises for relieving stress, increasing concentration, and revitalizing the body, mind, and senses.

Skillful Means: Gentle Ways to Successful Work. How to reawaken the joy of working and develop inner resources to create a successful, meaningful way of life.

Hidden Mind of Freedom. Clear, intimate talks remove barriers to self-understanding and show ways to activate the healing qualities of mind. Includes chapters on self-observation, emotions and balance, self-image, love and compassion.

Knowledge of Freedom: Time to Change. A unique biography of human experience, from the broadly historical to the intimate, often hidden, realm of the "I." A liberating perspective on self, world, and knowledge; provocative and challenging.

If you order Dharma books directly from the publisher, it will help us to make more such books available. Write for a free catalogue and new book announcements.

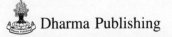 Dharma Publishing

2425 Hillside Avenue, Berkeley, California 94704 USA